MANAGING MULTI-DISCIPLINARY TEAMS
IN THE NHS

PAUL GORMAN

**KOGAN
PAGE**

YOURS TO HAVE AND TO HOLD
BUT NOT TO COPY

First published in 1998

Kogan Page Limited
120 Pentonville Road
London
N1 9JN

© Paul Gorman, 1998

British Library Cataloguing in Publication Data

A CIP record for this book is available from the British Library.

ISBN 0 7494 2787 6

Typeset by Kogan Page
Printed and bound in Great Britain by Biddles Ltd,
Guildford and King's Lynn

Contents

Contents

Contents

Foreword

Management can have a bad name in the NHS. We spend less of our budget on management than any comparable service and even that amount is being driven down. As the numbers of general managers in trusts are reduced, currently through a spate of mergers, more and more clinical time is taken up by management duties. Operational staff such as heads of specialist services or care homes, district nurses, ward sisters/charge nurses and their deputies find that they are increasingly expected to deal with management issues. The same issues that they were expected to refer to more senior staff just a few years ago.

The Healthcare Management Series is aimed at all staff who are involved in this process. People who have always thought of themselves as managers now find they must delegate more and more of their role as they take on ever broader responsibilities. Meanwhile those who see themselves primarily as providers of care find they must lead and support a team of others, allocate scarce resources and make difficult judgements about priorities if a high quality service is to be maintained. Basic training probably hasn't covered this; short courses on management may have been useful, but there is so much more to learn before feeling confident in this new role.

The writers of all the books in this series have been chosen for their practical experience of dealing with issues in the NHS and their ability to explain and illustrate the topics in a way which front line staff will appreciate. They are not, therefore, academic treatises but working handbooks full of advice and practical aids. More general books on management usually fail to reflect the particular features of the NHS, which make working in it both a joy and a frustration. The tribalism, the dominance of 'professionalism' and the commitment to the process of actually serving patients (rather than making a profit from them) which are such important drivers and which must be understood and harnessed if the service is to be well managed.

Multi-disciplinary working has always existed in healthcare, just as it does in most other walks of life. It is therefore not immediately obvious why this should be such a major issue at the present time. Changes in the acceptability of hierarchical structures in general and the growing emphasis of team working in management thinking, are two of the social trends that are causing a re-examination of working methods. The major structural changes in the way care is delivered, closer to the patient's home through a variety of agencies, has further emphasized the need for slick team work and healthy inter-personal and inter-agency working.

Multi-disciplinary healthcare teams have been defined variously (and tongue in cheek) as 'a group of people united by their intention to keep others off their patch' or 'a group of self actualizing professionals told what to do by a doctor'. Such cynicism has grown up as a defence among people who are not satisfied with the current status quo in their work teams. They know that things could be better. They know too that for improvements to occur there often has to be a shift of power away from certain individuals towards others in the group and there is much discomfort at the prospect of trying to bring this about. There is a natural reluctance to engage in confrontation of others, especially as it may damage working relationships, making work more difficult instead of easier. Paul Gorman's success in this book has been to combine a sound theoretical description of teams and team working with an honest and practical acknowledgement of life as a team member and team leader. Concepts and observations are illustrated throughout with short case studies and cameos, often drawn from his own experience as well as from published works.

My team has already begun to benefit from applying his ideas and to enjoy pointing out to me my own bad habits. This book should provide valuable advice to all team leaders on how to build and maintain a strong, working team and to all team members on how to contribute to joint success.

Keith Holdaway
Head of Training and Development
Mayday Healthcare NHS Trust, Croydon

Introduction

There are two dynamics at work in the delivery of health care in the National Health Service. First, the increasing specialization among clinicians as technology and our knowledge of the human body expand. Second, there is an increasing understanding that the patient is not simply the sum total of their symptoms. The whole person has to be worked with and the different specialisms need to work together to provide that care. The complexity of this task cannot be under-estimated. While writing this book I undertook a small personal case study of multi-disciplinary working. I had a lump in my scalp which, after extensive testing, was diagnosed as benign. A small, everyday intervention for the NHS. However, this happily successful intervention involved some 45 staff working in two general practices and two NHS Trusts. I visited five different departments on three separate sites. I saw two consultants, three registrars, one SHO, one general practitioner, two practice receptionists, two practice nurses, four departmental receptionists, four staff nurses, at least five health care assistants, several radiographers and a medical photographer. A porter gave me helpful directions when I got lost in the bowels of the Bristol Royal Infirmary. I also spoke on the phone with several secretaries and appointment clerks. In addition, I had two biopsies, a CT scan and chest x-ray, bone marrow and several blood samples. These were analysed by pathologists working in two separate laboratories.

Combining this array of multi-disciplinary talent and expertise into effective teams for patient care is what this book is about. Happily, my care team communicated well with each other and respected each other's contribution. The links between them were well maintained and did not appear to be jaundiced by organizational or professional conflict. Would that this were the case throughout the NHS. But, sadly, too many multi-disciplinary workplaces are dominated by organizational and professional jealousies and conflict. They are undermined by a weak sense of the processes at work beneath the surface.

Managers of multi-disciplinary teams, like all managers, have to balance the demands of the organization with the dynamics of the team and the desires of individual team members. This book is about trying to find that balance. Crucially, this that can only be forged through people. In making multi-disciplinary teams work, the most important skills are the inter-personal ones. We know how fragile egos and relationships can be, particularly in an environment that is as stressful and busy as the NHS. Mistakes get made, toes trodden on.

It is important not to be paralysed by the complexity of the situation. The search for the perfect solution can get in the way of reasonable progress. I am a great believer in good enough management. This is concerned with the central task of keeping the show on the road and the accumulation of small advantages which improve performance. This book provides a range of analytical frameworks and practical techniques to make this happen.

When I began writing this book I circulated a number of questionnaires round colleagues in the service and organized a number of small discussion groups. I asked about people's experience of working in multi-disciplinary teams and what advice they would offer to a new manager of a multi-discipli-nary team. While the sample was not very large and it was not scientifically weighted, the consensus of views spoke volumes. Far and away the most important factor for my respondents in making multi-disciplinary teams effective was an environment of mutual respect, openness and sharing. And the advice most commonly suggested to a new manager was value your staff and encourage them to value each other.

The book begins with an overview of multi-disciplinary working. In Chapters 2 and 3 I look at teams and in particular multi-disciplinary teams and how they work. Chapters 4 and 5 look at leadership and management and how they are, in fact, two sides of the same coin. Chapters 6 to 8 look at three crucial areas for a manager of a multi-disciplinary team: the ability to set goals and identify roles; communication in a multi-disciplinary multi-language context; and the importance of organizational and professional culture to performance. Chapter 9 discusses how to manage dysfunctional teams and difficult people. Chapter 10 looks at the importance of reflecting on practice to develop from being a good enough manager to becoming a getting better manager. Chapter 11 looks at the increasingly important world of multi-agency working. Finally, the Afterword pulls the main themes together.

Many people have contributed to the writing of this book and the development of the ideas that lie behind it. In particular I would like to thank the following: Helen Nicholson and her colleagues at Central Nottinghamshire NHS Trust; Nicola Rowen and her colleagues at Dudley Priority Care; Chris Bamford and her colleagues on the *Who Cares Wins* programme at Frenchay NHS Trust; all those who participated in the survey and focus groups; the general practices involved in the PUNS and STUNS programme in West London; the *Health Service Journal* and Health Education Authority for permission to reproduce material from their publications; my colleagues Glenda Taylor, David Wright and Louise Buckle for their timely advice and assistance; my wife Avril for her enthusiasm and suggestions and finally our dog Paxman with whom I discussed many of these issues during our morning walks.

Chapter 1

Multi-disciplinary Working in the NHS

Introduction

Modern health care is built upon a multi-disciplinary approach. Teams are one of the most effective organizational forms for bringing together the wisdom and skills of the various disciplines. So multi-disciplinary teams are a linchpin of effective health care. Anyone who has worked on a ward or in a general practice will know that realizing this simple proposition is anything but easy.

There is no one right way to manage a multi-disciplinary team. As we will discuss, multi-disciplinary teams in the NHS come in all sorts of shapes, sizes and settings. This book sets out to develop your ability to handle the variety of teams you will be working with. We will be focusing on three main themes:

- Developing your own understanding of yourself.
- Developing your understanding of how teams work.
- Increasing the range of techniques that you can use with your team.

In particular, I will argue that to manage a multi-disciplinary team effectively it is necessary to recognize and work with the strength of difference. The very nature of multi-disciplinary teams means bringing together different expertise, different value systems and different organizational hierarchies. Your task is to ensure that in your team these differences are a source of strength not the reason for weakness and division.

Much of what we will discuss can be transferred into a uni-disciplinary context. However, we are focusing particularly on managing teams in a multi-disciplinary context. This opening chapter maps this world and highlights the factors which we will be returning to throughout the rest of the book. It looks at the following:

- why we have different disciplines;
- how different disciplines impact on team working;
- the changing world in which these disciplines and teams are working.

Why Have Different Disciplines?

Sooner or later as the frustrations of multi-disciplinary or multi-agency working become too great, the cry is heard: 'wouldn't it be easier if we got rid of these barriers and everyone was the same?' The generic versus specialist debate has been going on for years and will continue for years to come. Specialization is a very human characteristic. We are inquisitive animals constantly exploring and learning about our world. We have learnt that specialization enables us to know more about things. This greater depth of knowledge gives us greater control over that part of our world. At the same time, other people have specialist knowledge about other things. If we come together we will have greater breadth of knowledge. It began with me knowing about stones and you knowing about wood so that together we could build a better shelter. Now it has developed into me knowing about psychology and you knowing about biology so that together we can treat this patient more effectively.

In health care, as in other areas of applied intelligence, we have arranged this knowledge into distinct disciplines. This has enabled knowledge to be organized and developed further. However, it is not simply knowledge which is divided by the boundaries of profession and discipline. Status, reward and power are also divided. For example, doctors get paid more than nurses and, in some environments, have more status and power.

Gender too plays a crucial role in the way professions operate internally and the way they interact with each other.

This duality of both developing the knowledge of the profession and defending its boundaries is often written into the mission statements of the professional bodies. For example, the British Medical Association seeks to 'promote medicine and allied sciences and to maintain the honour and interests of the medical profession' and the Royal College of Midwives seeks to 'promote the art and science of midwifery and to protect the interests of midwives'.

What Are Professions?

In some respects, professionals are not like ordinary citizens. They have been invested with particular rights and responsibilities. They have the power to intervene in the lives of others in ways which could lead to criminal charges for an ordinary citizen. Traditionally, these rights have been granted to professionals on a self-managing basis. That is, individuals will take responsibility for their own actions and the management of their work load within clear ethical boundaries.

The boundaries around these rights and responsibilities have been carefully drawn, usually by statute. The theme of the self-managing professional continues with part of the role of the professional bodies being to police these boundaries and to protect the public from charlatans. The professional bodies act as gatekeepers to the professions, thus controlling the right to practise.

Individual practitioners are proud of their professional status and rightly so. The professions and the bodies that control them have made a huge contribution to the development of knowledge about our health and the best way to practise. Getting into a profession is a slow and often difficult process. It builds in people a very powerful sense of being someone apart, whether they are a nurse, a doctor or an anaesthetist. This professionalism is one of most important factors in determining how multi-disciplinary teams work and we will be returning to it throughout this book. For now, I simply want to underline the felt nature of this professionalism. This is partly the warm glow factor of being part of a great human enterprise, but more practically it is, as the UKCC describes it, being 'confident and competent' to act.

My wife retrained some years ago and became a lawyer. For me it was a fascinating case study of someone acquiring the characteristics of a profession. I realized something fundamental had happened when she suddenly began haranguing a solicitor on *Eastenders* for unprofessional practice. Teachers on courses leading to professional qualifications report that it takes only a few weeks before students begin acquiring the attitudes that colour the professions so deeply, with comments from doctors like, 'It's OK, she's a doctor' or for nurses 'only nurses really understand'. This process is sometimes rather grandly called becoming encultured. That is the process by which individuals acquire the attitudes and behaviours, the mind-set, which mark one group off from another.

As these students progress through their courses, they learn the overt parts of being a doctor or a nurse. They learn about the different elements of the patient's condition and a set of responses that are based on different sets of values. When they look at a patient they are looking for different things and will deploy a different set of treatment techniques. However, there is a paradox which cuts to the heart of multi-disciplinary working: the stronger the internal identity and cohesion of the group, the more difficult the management of external relationships becomes.

While the boundaries around our role and responsibilities are stable, all parties can proceed with confidence. However, one constant of the NHS is change. Organizations merge, departments are restructured, the skill mix in teams is manipulated, and so on. Even if we set aside issues of status, power and job security which we know to be hugely important factors in determining an individual's response to change, the change will impact at a deeper level. The certainty about the boundaries of our role becomes eroded. This prompts questions in the mind of the professional: 'am I exceeding my authority?', 'am I carrying out my role properly?'. The professional is no longer grounded in the certainty of knowing what their profession is and is not or where the boundaries of other professions now lie. Furthermore, there is a perception amongst many professionals that their right to self-management is being increasingly constrained and challenged by their employing organizations.

These professional cultures and mind-sets are an enormously powerful factor. Your job as a manager of a multi-disciplinary team is to engage with them and to draw the best out of them for your patients and your staff.

At this point you may be wondering why this book is not called managing multi-professional teams. As I have argued above, the professions have an element of exclusivity about them. This exclusivity is thought by many professionals and organizations to be unhelpful in the provision of high quality care. If we describe our team as multi-professional, where does that leave the non-professional members of staff like the auxiliaries, receptionists, porters and the rest? These are the people who often have the highest level of contact with the patient. And most important, where does it leave the patient and their family? For these reasons this book is about multi-disciplinary teams.

The Changing World of Medicine and the NHS

The world in which all this activity is taking place is changing fast. The main themes will be well known to you as practitioners in the field. There is an increasing demand for NHS services driven partly by the ageing population and partly by increasing patient expectations. Hardly a day goes by without a new wonder drug or procedure being announced to the world and the strides that have been made in the last 40 years or so are breathtaking. Anything, it seems, is possible. In the NHS this expansion of patient expectations has been fuelled by the introduction of initiatives like the Patient's Charter which have reinforced the message about individual choice.

The increase in possibilities for individuals has not been matched by a collective will to commit sufficient resources to health care. Restrictions on resources are the daily reality of the NHS and the management of difficult choices about the use of those resources is the everyday stuff of your job.

The informed patient now has the whole of the Internet to call upon. This is only one aspect of the impact of new technology. At the leading edge, bio-technology offers dazzling prospects. Telemedicine can bring world expertise direct to your local health centre. Decision support software, making use of the dispassionate objectivity of the computer, is already being trialled by a number of ambulance trusts to improve the effectiveness of their responses. How long before other forms of assessment and triage are supported by software?

We are already seeing the increasing use of protocols within health care to aid consistency and quality. It is only a short step for these to be loaded onto a computer. If the task of remembering detailed medical knowledge is increasingly taken over by computers, what role then remains for the individual autonomous practitioner exercising their professional judgement? 'We have hugely qualified staff, do we need all these protocols?', asks one doctor. A cash-strapped employer might turn the question around and ask 'with all these protocols, do we need all these hugely qualified staff?' Skill mix, or as it is sometimes more cynically described grade mix, is going to be the critical human resource issue in the NHS over the next ten years.

Multi-disciplinary teams will be right at the heart of these changes. All of these factors are combining to threaten the idea of the autonomous professional carrying on a vocation in the way they have done for much of this century. Disillusionment and uncertainty about their role and self-perception make professionals increasingly defensive.

Furthermore. multi-disciplinary working is actually a spectrum of relationships which range from loosely coordinated collaborative efforts through to tightly organized teams. Most health care professionals are required to work at multiple points along this spectrum, depending on the particular needs of their patient, often assuming different responsibilities during the same day.

All in all, it is a complex and unstable brew which can seem overwhelming at times. However, help is at hand. There is a widely accepted model of multi-disciplinary working which draws these themes together and which gives you a starting point for your management approach.

The Three Dimensions of Multi-disciplinary Working

There are three dimensions to multi-disciplinary working which as a manager you need to be aware of and work with. These dimensions are shown in Figure 1.1.

- The structural dimension.
- The cultural dimension.
- The interpersonal dimension.

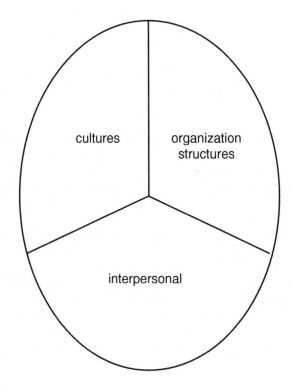

Figure 1.1 Effectiveness in a multi-disciplinary team

The structural aspects of multi-disciplinary working spring from issues such as differing levels of autonomy for members of the team, the differing lines of accountability, differing pay levels, differing organizational status, and so forth. The structural aspects of multi-disciplinary working are typically about formal organizational issues.

The cultural aspects of multi-disciplinary working spring from the differing professional rationales of members of the team, the tensions between the different ideologies and value systems which underpin the professions. Each profession working in health care is trained to look at the patient through a very particular pair of spectacles. They see particular things and give weight to different pieces of information.

The interpersonal aspects of multi-disciplinary working spring from our similarities and differences as humans. That uncanny knack we have of knowing almost instantly whether we will get on with someone. Difficulties which arise from the structural or cultural dimensions may be wrongly attributed to someone being difficult to work with.

You will appreciate that these three dimensions are not free-standing or autonomous. For example, we know that gender is a very important issue in the way multi-disciplinary teams work. There are elements of gender which are structural (men generally earn more than women), cultural (men will often cast women into caring roles) and interpersonal (some men prefer to work with men, some with women and the same is true for women).

We act as we do as a result of the interplay of our position in the organizational hierarchy, the professional culture within which we work and our own personality. However, this model is helpful in offering a way of disentangling and understanding what is going on in front of you. If you can correctly diagnose the problem, it will make a successful solution more likely. Because of the interconnected nature of the three dimensions, a single hit solution focusing, for example, only on the structural is less likely to succeed than one which seeks to address all three dimensions. It has been argued many times that one of the reasons that organizational restructurings are often only partially successful is that they themselves are only partial. They tackle issues of formal structures, reporting lines and so forth, but they do not address the cultural aspects nor the personal behaviours which can help to make the change effective.

The basic model as presented is static. In real life, the situation is dynamic and fluid. Organizations are often restructuring, merging, delayering and so on. Professional cultures are also shifting. In nursing, for example, the move towards nurses being graduate recruits or achieving degrees as mature students is setting up a new interface with other professions and within nursing itself. And people's lives change. The birth of a child or death of a partner, for example, will change the way any individual reacts to a given work situation.

As the balance of forces which interact in a multi-disciplinary team moves, so the team and the way it works together will move. Generally peoples' reaction to change is to head for the familiar and the trusted. Because, sadly, the vast bulk of professional training is done in a uni-disciplinary environment, this often takes teams away from the multi-disciplinary approach which is such a strength for patient care. This means that the multi-disciplinary approach does not just happen by itself. It is the result of a collective act of will. The single most important factor in making multi-disciplinary working effective is staff commitment. And it is your responsibility, as the manager of a multi-disciplinary team, to make that act of will happen. You have to argue for and organize a multi-disciplinary approach. You have to encourage it, nurture it and monitor its state of health.

> As long as you keep the improvement of health and health care at the centre, a lot of the multi-professional stuff falls away.
>
> (Dr Linda Headrick Professor of Medicine,
> Case Weston Reserve University, USA)

Given all of this, are multi-disciplinary teams worth the effort?

The Benefits of Multi-disciplinary Teams

It is possible to identify five core benefits from multi-disciplinary working.

- Better quality decisions – diagnostic and treatment issues can be highly complex and serious. By using all the information from all the team there is less danger of decisions being taken in ignorance of vital data.
- Clear roles and responsibilities – the allocation of roles and responsibilities is transparent and understood where all team members are together in a team meeting.
- Greater commitment to the care plan – ownership of decisions is better when people have participated in the choice of treatment.

- One team, one voice – the whole team is working to a single treatment plan and is speaking with one voice to the patient and their family. There are few things more disturbing to patients and their families than team members disagreeing over treatment.
- Mutual support and encouragement – team members can be a source of support and encouragement to each other in environments which are often stressful and pressurized.

Conclusion

When it works well, multi-disciplinary working offers better treatment for patients and a better quality of working life for the practitioners. Multi-disciplinary teams are exciting and rewarding places to work. Successful multi-disciplinary teams report higher morale and greater job satisfaction. Your task is to successfully find a way through this complex and shifting web of organizational intrigue, patient aspiration and financial constraints. It is not impossible, although it isn't easy. The first step is to be aware of the complexity of things you are working with, but to not allow that to paralyse your ability to act and lead. The model of multi-disciplinary working gives you a framework in which to organize yourself. You will need to address the following:

- Structural aspects of multi-disciplinary working – do people understand the overall goal and their roles and responsibilities? Are they rewarded by the organization for working in a multi-disciplinary way? Are issues of status and power getting in the way of a multi-disciplinary approach? Are the reporting lines appropriate? And so forth.
- Cultural aspects of multi-disciplinary working – is there a view in your team and the organization as a whole that this is the right way to work? Are divisive manifestations of professional culture tolerated? Is there a flag around which all members of the team can rally?
- Inter-personal aspects of multi-disciplinary working – are people clear how they relate to each other? Do they know the sorts of behaviours that you are trying to encourage? On a

personal level, how well are they handling the changes to their role? And so on.

Later chapters in this book will explore these issues in more depth and provide some additional analytical frameworks and techniques that you can use. They will also discuss the extent to which you as the manager have to make this happen and the extent to which you are trying to create a set of conditions in which people can do it for themselves. Achieving the levels of effectiveness that you want from your team, in spite of all the problems and difficulties, is what the rest of this book is about.

Chapter 2

Teams and Networks

Introduction

Teams form the backbone of organizations. Team working is seen to be the standard model by which organizations deliver results. Staff expect to work in teams and patients expect to be treated by staff working in teams. The rhetoric of organizations echoes with exhortations to work in teams. And yet it often seems our teams are less effective than they ought to be. This is not a new phenomena. Caius Petronious writing about the Roman Army in AD 66 said:

> We trained hard, but it seemed that every time we were beginning to form up into teams we would be re-organized. I was to learn later in life that we tend to meet any situation by re-organizing, and a wonderful method it can be for creating the illusion of progress, while producing confusion, inefficiency and demoralization.

Sadly, in the last 2 000 years we do not seem to have got much better at managing teams.

The next two chapters explore teams, in particular multi-disciplinary teams, and how you can help build them. In this chapter we will look at teams in general. Many of the issues we will discuss are as true for uni-disciplinary teams as they are for multi-disciplinary teams. In particular we will look at the following:

- why we have teams;
- what a team is;
- teams in the NHS;
- size, teams and networks;
- what makes teams successful.

Why Have Teams?

Teams have both practical and psychological aspects to them. Teams bring individuals together to achieve more than they can separately. Teams also appeal to us because we are naturally clubbable creatures. We seek comfort and enjoyment from each other. We like to work with other people to achieve things. And we like to have our contribution acknowledged.

For every one of us the thing that is most difficult about teams is that they cannot be made up of clones of ourselves. The whole point about teams is that they bring together individuals with a blend of skills, knowledge, opinions, personalities and thinking styles. The next chapter will look at these differences in detail.

All of us have an ambivalent relationship with the team. We want the team to succeed and understand that our individuality will be submerged for the greater good, but there are limits. We also want to retain that which makes us distinctive. The dilemma between what is good for the team and what is good for the individual is the one that you as manager will have to balance for each member of your team. To help you do that you will need a map to be able to make sense of what you are seeing in front of you.

What is a Team?

Now this might seem a rhetorical question. We all know what a team is. A team is a collection of people working towards a common goal. However, that definition could also apply to a committee and you wouldn't have bought this book if you thought it was about committee building. Michael West and Julie Slater (1996) have suggested that there are four characteristics of a team. These are as follows:

- Collective responsibility for achieving shared aims and objectives.
- Members must interact with each other in order to achieve those objectives.
- Members have a more or less defined role, at least some of which are differentiated from each other.
- The team has an identity as a team.

The use of the word 'member' in this list is significant. A team has a clear boundary. There are people who are in the team and people who are outside it. It is this which gives it an identity as a team and marks it off from an *ad hoc* working group. It also emphasizes the fact that teams are made up of individuals who collectively share responsibility. Membership carries implications about what is expected of individuals by their colleagues. The reciprocal expectation of authority and participation is not explicit, but is one of the key issues in team working, particularly for junior members.

Teams in the NHS

By using West and Slater's criteria to examine three multi-disciplinary teams in the NHS we can reveal one of the most important confusions about multi-disciplinary teams: the gap between the reality of how the team operates and our expectations of how a team should work. We will look at the following:

- an operating theatre team;
- a ward team;
- a primary health care team.

They may all be described as teams but how they work and the individual roles of their members are very different.

In an operating theatre the team will usually have no more than half a dozen members. They will all be present throughout the length of the operation. During their contact with this patient they will normally see no others. Each member of the team, whether they are a surgeon, anaesthetist or nurse, will have a clearly defined role which they will have practised frequently, often together. Communication is instantaneous. The patient's case is acute and urgent. If help or advice is required from outside the team, it will be sought and provided immediately.

A ward team will be typically made up of four nurses and often a ward clerk. However, the personnel in the team will change during the day as shifts hand over. Permanent staff may be supplemented by bank or agency staff. The boundaries of the team are not clearly defined as in the operating theatre: do the porters count as team members? Are the junior doctors and or the consultants included? What about PAMs? Roles within the team will be clearly defined. Communication is both instantaneous and delayed. For example, it will also need to be made across boundaries such as shift changes and to other departments. The team is looking after a number of patients at one time, all located in the same place. Some of these patients may be on the ward for only a few hours, others for several days. Patients are mainly conscious and the more active ones may 'help out' by chatting to their neighbours.

A primary health care team can be made up of up to 50 or 60 people, who may convene together as a group only rarely. Patients are dispersed across a wide area in a variety of settings. Communication between team members is often difficult. Roles can be blurred particularly along the health and social care boundary. Staff are treating individual patients often for long periods of time. Typically, patients will only see one team member at a time, although they may see several during the course of a single day. Not all patients will be seen by all team members.

Three health care units which are described as teams, but are three very different structures. As we have seen, all three teams meet the first two of West and Slater's criteria. Their members have to interact to achieve their goals (although they may not be treating the same patient at the same time) and all members have distinct roles.

In respect of West and Slater's criteria of shared objectives, an operating theatre team has a very specific goal: to successfully perform the operation. However, for the ward team and the primary health care team, while the objectives may be shared, they will be looser: to treat and care for the patient. The more people involved in the multi-disciplinary team, the looser the shared objective becomes. Individual members of the team may have specific goals, for example to deliver this patient to the discharge room on time, to treat this patient for pneumonia, to record accurately a blood pressure, but the shared objective has to be more loosely defined.

Likewise, conformance to West and Slater's final criteria of an identity as a team. We have noted above both the ward and primary health care teams have soft membership boundaries. Only the operating theatre has a clearly defined membership and therefore a clear identity.

In summary, then, the operating theatre is clearly a team according to West and Slater's criteria but both the ward and primary health care teams lack some of the basic ingredients. And yet they do have some of the characteristics and people call them teams. This is a muddle and one that we need to explore and understand before we can begin to work with these units successfully.

Size, Teams and Networks

Titanic teams

One of the most striking elements of the results of the questionnaires I circulated when researching for this book were the sizes of team that some respondents said they were working in. They ranged from half-dozen up to teams as large as 70, 80 and in one case more than 90. The issues which will emerge in these teams, particularly of participation and communication will be very different.

There is an old saying that the best committee has two members, one of whom is ill. It can feel a bit like that with teams. Most of the standard text books describe the optimal size for a team as being between 6 and 12. As teams grow in size, so they find it increasingly difficult to meet West and Slater's four characteristics. Collective responsibility for achieving shared aims becomes weakened as individuals or sub-groups take responsibility for their own piece of the jigsaw of care. Interactions between members will decline as communications are channelled through more formal structures such as department heads and sub-group leaders. In teams of increasing size people will still have defined roles, but often the identity of the team becomes blurred and the identity of the organization or department takes over.

So where have these titanic teams of 60-plus sprung from? They are magnificent in conception. They reflect a holistic view of the treatment of the patient and the complexity of modern health care. Even relatively simple interventions involve a large number of people making a contribution to the care of a patient from receptionists, through to the nurses, health care assistants, doctors, laboratory staff, medical technicians, porters, catering staff, and so on. The idea of a titanic team stems from the commitment of clinicians to seeing their patient through their total care. It recognizes that the patient's experience of their care will be coloured by the contributions of all of these individuals and groups. This is obviously the case. However, it does not make these individuals and groups into a team.

I think these assemblages of people are called teams because it is the politically correct way to describe the way we wish to be seen to be working rather than because it reflects the reality of the relationships. A team carries with it an expectation of a degree of cohesion and integration which is hugely difficult to sustain over such large numbers of people. Inevitably, in titanic teams status in the hierarchy is the real bestower of authority and the reciprocity which is implicit in teams is weak.

We have already seen that as size increases so conformance to West and Slater's characteristics of a team weakens. Let us now test these titanic teams against the four characteristics of a successful team. They can meet the task and the organizational agenda. But communication is often difficult and patchy and they fail to address the human elements of team building, the sense of belonging and co-ownership, that good teams provide. People are motivated by being able to see how their contribution makes a difference and by having that contribution recognized by colleagues

So we have organizational units operating in the NHS that are called teams but lack many of the basic features of a team, and more importantly, of successful teams. Expectations are raised amongst staff that are very difficult to meet.

There are two concepts which are helpful in untangling this mess. These are vertical integration and networking.

Vertical integration

Vertical integration is an organizational idea that has emerged from economics and the study of how businesses have structured themselves. Vertical integration occurs when one company integrates within itself many or all of the activities needed to provide its final service or product. An example from history would be the Ford motor company who owned a steel works and rubber factory as well as their car plants. Ford owned and directly controlled every part of the production process in a single hierarchy run from Detroit. From around the 1930s to the 1970s this type of massive integrated corporation under the control of a single leader was the dominant organizational form in the private sector.

It seems to me that this vertical integration is what the concept of the titanic team is striving for: a single organizational unit, a gigantic production line, under the control of one person which is responsible for all of the care received by a patient. However, it fails to take account of the differing lines of accountability that staff in the NHS have. A district nurse is not accountable in management terms to a GP, but to the manager in a Trust. A radiographer is not directly accountable to a surgeon. Moreover, large corporations are now moving away from the model of vertical integration as they have found it discourages personal responsibility, innovation and flexibility.

Networks

At the other end of the of the spectrum of organizational forms is the complex, multi-contact network. Networks have become one of the buzz phrases of recent years. They are interconnected groups of people or organizations and their purpose is to provide mutual benefit. This benefit may be the sharing of information, support and advice or introductions to other people.

Networks are not hierarchical and have no boundaries. They are held together by personal relationships. Networks can be dispersed over huge areas. Networks are maintained through use and communication. Many common activities can be described as networking. Here are a few examples:

- ringing someone for a chat;
- attending a conference;
- sending a Christmas or birthday card.

The growth of electronic communication and the Internet are providing enormous scope for developing new connections.

People never formally join a network, but there is often a shared experience or time together that allows the basic level of trust and knowledge to develop. People you studied with, people you have worked with, people you have played sport with. They are your friends, family and work colleagues.

A network is more than just a circle of friends and acquaintances. It is the second order of contacts that networks provide that makes them different from your mates down the pub. My network is not just the people I know. It is all the people they know. Your network can act as your sponsor when you make contact with a stranger. All of us have networks, just some of us are better at using them than others. Your network is one of the most powerful assets that you have at your disposal. As well as being a source of strength and cohesion, networks can work to exclude groups or individuals on the basis of sex, race or belief, either consciously or not.

Many of the world's most successful companies now organize themselves as strategic or business networks. A strategic network is an arrangement by which companies set up a web of close relationships that form a system geared to the provision of a product or service in a coordinated way. In a strategic network, one company takes the role of 'central controller' acting as the customer's champion organizing the flow of goods and information among many other independent companies to ensure that the final client gets exactly what they are supposed to get in an efficient way. Thus McDonald's or Marks & Spencer will be very precise in the way they specify exactly what they want their suppliers to provide (for example, the type of potato seed, the precise weave of a cardigan) but they do not own those supplier companies or concern themselves particularly about how they organize themselves so long as they deliver what they are supposed to.

This seems to me to be a better description of the way the NHS actually runs. Small groups or teams of professionals taking responsibility for their own actions with a central player, who will normally be the patient's doctor acting as gatekeeper in accessing the services. These networks can be thought of as coalitions of care.

You can see that this idea of a team is a slippery one in the NHS, with one word being used to describe a multiplicity of different organizational concepts. When you have individuals trying to work together but each carrying a different understanding and expectation of what is likely to occur: one perhaps informed by the model of an integrated team of half a dozen, another with a model of the vertical integration of large numbers of people and the third with a model of a network or coalition of care, you can imagine the difficulties and tensions that lie ahead. Part of your job as a manager is to understand what is going on in front of you and to explain it to your staff and colleagues. Multi-disciplinary teams require a shared understanding to work effectively.

What Makes a Team Successful?

There are five factors which characterize successful teams.

- Clear goals – I know what we are supposed to be doing.
- Clear roles – I know what my job is in achieving those goals.
- Right mix to deliver the results – I have the skills and knowledge to do this part, you have the skills and knowledge to do that.
- Not a lot of ego, a good process, trust between team members – there is good internal communication and you can rely on me to do what I say I'm going to do.
- It works for the individuals in the team – there is something in the goals of the team or the way we work together which I feel is of benefit to me.

In the short term it is possible to overcome weaknesses in all areas bar one: clear goals. If the goals are clear, we can muddle through on who does what. If the goals are clear, it is usually possible to make do and mend with gaps in skill or knowledge or to bring in what's required. If the goals are clear, we can overcome a poor team process or communication especially if we have a strong leader, to which we will return later. If the goals are clear, team members will put up with lack of benefits to themselves providing they buy into the team's goals. But in the long term all of these characteristics need to be present to make a team effective.

A health authority I was working with had run into a problem with some of the locality groups it had set up. The health authority had never been very clear about the purpose of these groups except that it wanted to be seen to be doing something. For one group of GPs the opportunity to meet together once every couple of months and to share problems was enormously helpful and the meetings were always well attended. Cohesion amongst the group was high. However, the health authority was struggling to figure out what it was getting for its money other than happier GPs. The solution was to give the group a set of questions that the health authority wanted a view on (a specific task) and to feed these questions in over two or three meetings so that the cohesion which the group/team had developed was not disrupted but was turned to a useful purpose for the health authority.

The list of success criteria above is not in any particular order of importance. However, the different weight team members attach to each of these factors tends to differ depending on their seniority within the organization. By and large, the more senior you are in the organization, the more importance you attach to the existence of clearly defined goals. The more junior you are in the organization, the more importance you attach to the existence of some personal benefit in your team membership. This is often articulated as wanting to have your views respected. To feel, in other words, that you are a valued member of the team. This is the task – people continuum we will discuss in more detail in Chapter 4. You have to find the balance between the two in your team and your organization.

Conclusion

Teams are the basic building blocks of organizations. They are so important that the label 'team' is often attached to organizational forms which do not meet any of the characteristics of a team, let alone ones that perform successfully. This mislabelling is a problem because a team is an organizational form which sets up very particular expectations about how it will operate. The dissonance of expectation and performance can set up all sorts of tensions which you as the manager of the team will need to handle. You will do this through managing people and building a common understanding of what your team is about.

Chapter 3

Building a Multi-disciplinary Team

Introduction

Teams are only groups of individuals working together more or less effectively. To really get into teams, you need to really get into people and figure out what pushes their buttons individually and collectively. It is simultaneously the most exciting, bewildering and frustrating part of any manager's job.

In the last chapter we looked at structural issues in teams. In this chapter we look at people in teams, how they work together and begin to look at welding those individuals into an effective unit. In particular, we will look at the following aspects:

- the life cycle of a team;
- the changing role of the manager in that life cycle;
- people in teams;
- are patients members of the team?
- the differences between multi-disciplinary and uni-disciplinary teams;
- the life cycle of collaborative enterprises;
- taking stock of where your team is at present;
- where do you want them to be?

Together this basic geography of team dynamics and personal styles will give you the blueprint from which to start building your team.

Life Cycle of a Team

Overview

There is a well established formula first set out in the 1960s by B. Tuckman (Tuckman, 1965). Tuckman argues that teams have four phases in their life cycle, as shown in Figure 3.1.

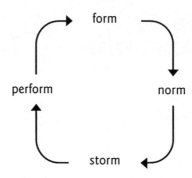

Figure 3.1 The basic life cycle of a team

The first phase is Form, getting to know each other, beginning to explore roles and the task. The next phase is Norm, developing formal or informal rules of conduct and behaviour which will govern the way they work together. The third phase is Storm where conflict between individuals about roles, priorities and relationships, which may have been bubbling under the surface, come out into the open. Finally, having cleared the air, the team Perform, carrying out the task efficiently and effectively with a high level of mutual support.

In a moment, I will go into each of these phases and how to diagnose where your team is in its development, but there are a couple of things to note. First, no team has ever progressed in neat straight lines taking each phase in turn. Team members are too capricious and human for anything so rational. Teams and the individuals that make them up will dot back and forth, norming one minute, forming the next. In addition, in most teams you will find sub-groups operating.

The same life cycle that operates in teams also operates in sub-groups. So you may have one sub-group of old hands who have been around for years who have done it all before and another sub-group of newcomers. The old hands will have normed and stormed down the years and will have a clear view about how things should be performed. The newcomers won't be as coherent as a group because they are still forming amongst themselves. So what you may see is a relatively tight sub-group of old hands and a loose collection of individual newcomers. As a manager you must expect to see overlapping behaviours like this and be nimble enough to cope with people in different stages of the cycle.

Second, there are some writers on teams who would change the order of life cycle and put storming before norming. You have to clear the air before you can write the rule book. My experience is that often the first thing a new team will do, and particularly one which is multi-disciplinary, is to work out expectations of behaviour and performance. Writing the rules is a pretty safe and sensible place to start. We can test out each other's position in an abstract and relatively non-threatening way. As the team begins to develop, their norms often act as the focus for the team's storming. For example, it is much easier for me to express my anger about the general standard of time-keeping in a team meeting than it is for me to confront you directly about your timekeeping.

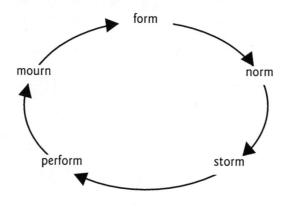

Figure 3.2 The extended life cycle of a team

Finally, I would add a fifth stage to the life cycle of the team. This is the stage of mourning (I am grateful to my colleague Glenda Taylor for pointing this out to me). Teams will often have a limited life. Either because they exist to execute a particular task or they get disrupted by the constant waves of reorganization and restructuring that wash through the NHS (see Figure 3.2).

Some years ago I was asked to do a team-building session with a multi-disciplinary and multi-agency team working in learning disability. The Trust and Social Service Department had decided to restructure the locality teams charged with improving learning disability services because all bar one had failed to make any impact. The team I was working with was the one that had worked well. So here I had a room full of people who got on well together, had worked well together and had delivered improvements on the ground who were now to be broken up because of the failings of others. As I talked to them about what they wanted, it became clear to me it wasn't a team-building session that was needed, it was a wake.

As people we often want closure in our life, the certainty that this period is now over and it's time to move on. We like to tie up the loose ends. Lots of teams fade away rather than being brought to a formal conclusion. The mourning stage provides the opportunity to express anger or sadness about the demise of the team. It also allows lessons to be drawn and successes to be celebrated. The overall effect is much more satisfactory than just stopping.

With those notes in mind, let's look at the five stages in the life of a team in more detail. How can you tell where your team is in the process? What can you do as the team manager to move them on?

Forming

Forming is characterized by considerable levels of anxiety and often hesitant participation. The discussion within the team will often be dominated by one or two powerful voices. The doubt in other members' minds will be: 'dare I open my mouth?', 'will they let me join in?'. There is degree of formality about these exchanges. When they introduce themselves people will often give an indication of their knowledge, experience: I am a social worker, I am a priest. This display of rank and position is typical of the introductory period. The more authority you have or claim to have, the more responsibility you are claiming for yourself.

The team will be looking to develop a joint understanding of what the task is. Attempts will be made to define the situation and this can often drift off into discussions of irrelevant issues and intellectualizing. There will be a lot of basic information exchanged. The team is trying to make a start.

As the team leader, your role in these early days is to be highly visible. You need to lead from the front. This may be as explicit as setting the task, but you should certainly be looking at steering the team towards the right goals. You should also encourage people to be clear in their views. If you don't understand what is being said or you suspect that others don't understand what's being said, ask a question. As a general rule, always encourage people to ask stupid questions. They are often exactly what is required. Keep an eye on the quiet team members and seek out ways of drawing them into the discussion. A gentle question like 'Is that your experience, Louise?' will often work better than something more direct like: 'What do you think?' Above all, don't try to rush or skip the forming stage. Once people feel confident who they are working with, they will work at a quicker tempo.

> The one piece of advice I would give to a new manager is always remember how hard it is to work with strangers.
>
> (Manager, Alcohol Service)

Norming

During the norming stage, the team will begin to gel together for the first time. Expectations of each other will become clearer. At this point it will become easier for you to recognize which of the team roles discussed later in this chapter individuals are beginning to play. Members will also begin to identify with the team.

As the team begins to emerge, so the plans will be drawn up and people will seek each other's opinions. Your role at this point is to step back a little and allow your team members the opportunity to take more of the initiative in talking and working with each other. Ensure that decisions about the task are recorded, together with how they will be achieved and the way that the team is expecting to work together. Norming will give you opportunities to catch people out doing the right things and to praise them for it. Reinforcing the behaviours you want will encourage people to do them again. It is a small trick of management, but a remarkably powerful one.

Storming

When a team is storming the emotional temperature rises as conflicts between individuals and sub-groups burst out into the open. You may well see defensiveness, competition and jealousy between your team members. Their attitude to you and your leadership may become more critical. Sometimes this emotion can be displaced into resisting the validity of the task and to the things that need to be done in order to achieve the task.

Your role in this phase is twofold. First, don't let the team panic that it's all falling apart. Second, don't panic yourself that it's all falling apart. Remind the team and yourself that conflict is good in a high performing team and that highly differentiated teams, that is ones made up of real differences of opinion, personality and expertise, are often the most effective as well as being the sparkiest. So be open with them and recognize together the stage you have reached. Teams have to go through the storming stage to become truly effective. You will also need to be there for all the members of the team particularly the ones lacking power or status. You can do this by giving people the opportunity to express their ideas and make them feel that their contribution is valued by you, the team manager, even if not by the rest of the group. Having your views listened to is a crucial part of feeling part of the team. Storming is when people can fall off or feel left out of the team. You need to hold the team together during this phase. Finally, you will need to draw a clear line between challenges to the views of others which are constructive and those which are destructive. Be clear with team members about what you will tolerate.

Performing

A performing team has a flow and cohesion about it. The roles people take on are clear but flexible. There is pragmatism in support of the task and good levels of mutual support. One of the classic signs of a performing team is that you are not the only team member praising good work.

The team will have a strong goal orientation and there will be insight and understanding about the part that each team member has in achieving it. You will sit back wishing it was always like this! Your task will be to oil the wheels ensuring that people keep up standards of performance, praising and drawing attention to achievements and to how far the team has come. But mainly your job is to keep out of the way and let your team get on with it.

Mourning

Members of cohesive teams that have worked well and that have been characterized by high levels of personal commitment and support are often reluctant to let them go. Members will invent additional tasks in order to sustain the team.

There are two important tasks to be completed in the mourning phase. One is to evaluate the effectiveness of the team and to try to draw the lessons so that the good can be reproduced and the bad left behind. The second is to record and celebrate the team's achievements both personal and collective. Your role in the mourning phase is:

- to ensure recognition that the team is coming to an end;
- to summarize the achievements;
- to allow people the opportunity to say goodbye.

One way to do this is to ask members individually for feedback on the following: which one thing they would like to carry away with them from the team?; and which one thing would they like to dump in the bin? Make them write them down on a piece of paper. Put the 'keeps' on a flip chart and the 'dumps' in a bin. It sounds corny, but it really does work!

The Changing Role of the Manager

Through the life cycle of the team the roles that you will play as team leader will shift quite markedly. Developing the ability to accurately gauge the needs of your team and the nimbleness to respond appropriately are two of the most important skills any team manager can have. Managing a team is a complex job, but it is also one of the most rewarding. If you pay attention to all the various strands, trust your instincts and learn from your successes and mistakes, you will get better at it.

Form	Leading, initiating the team's discussion. Focus on the task, Praising and rewarding appropriate behaviours
Norm	Chairing the team's discussion. Clarifying individual's positions and roles. Praising and rewarding appropriate behaviours
Storm	Referee of what is acceptable behaviour and views. Personal support to all members of the team. Praising and rewarding appropriate behaviours
Perform	Oiler of the wheels. Champion of the team's achievements. Evaluating the team's achievements. Drawing the team to a
Mourn	close. Praising and rewarding appropriate behaviours

Table 3.1 The changing role of the manager

Table 3.1 sets out the way the roles you will play will move through leader of the team in the forming stage, to chairing the team in the norming phase, to refereeing the team in the storming phase, to champion of the team in the performing phase to that of summarizer in the mourning phase. And all the time you will be maintaining the one-to-one relationships with the various personalities in your team and keeping an eye on the overall goal, budgets and time scales.

People in Teams

To help you find your way through this array of roles and circumstances I set out below two ways of reading the people in your team. These are based on these two aspects: how people behave in teams and how people think about the world they are working in. Using these typologies is beneficial because they give you a framework to help you do the following:

- understand what you are seeing in front of you;
- predict what may happen next;
- engage with your staff better.

Remember, an approach that engages one person won't necessarily connect with another. So use a variety of descriptions, methods, and techniques.

There are dozens of different approaches to understanding people in teams. I have chosen these two for a number of reasons. First, and most important, I find them useful for me. You may find that you get on better with one rather than the other. My view is try out a number of different approaches to diagnosing teams until you find a couple that you like and then stick with them. The benefit of any technique increases as you become more used to working with it and get better at interpreting what it is telling you. Second, these two approaches are looking at different aspects of people in teams: the way they act and the way they think. Clearly what we do and the way we think are linked but they represent two different ways for you to gain some purchase on the people you are working with.

First, I need to sound a note of warning. One of the problems with all typologies of people is that they can be interpreted too literally. Very few of us fit neatly into any single type. Our actions and thought processes will range across a wide spectrum of styles depending on the circumstances we find ourselves in. This is particularly the case when we are working in organizational teams where factors such as status and power within the organizational hierarchy will influence our actions. So don't be too literal in allocating people into little boxes.

Nevertheless, over time it is possible to discern biases in the way individuals behave and think. Being able to read these signals accurately is an enormous help for managers looking to find ways of connecting with the staff they are trying to motivate and lead. Good management, particularly in a multi-disciplinary team, is about starting where people are rather than where you would like them to be.

People in teams – a generic typology

The three main branches of behaviour in teams are:

- opening up and closing down;
- focusing on the team and focusing on the environment;
- introversion and extroversion.

Individual actions are made up of combinations of these three pairs of behaviours. To plot any specific action you need to think in three dimensions. Think of the corner of a room with the opening and closing axis running from floor to ceiling, the team and environment axis running along one wall from side to side and the introversion and extroversion axis running along the floor from front to back. Any one action could be plotted on all these three axes and would appear as a point in the space of the room (see Figure 3.3).

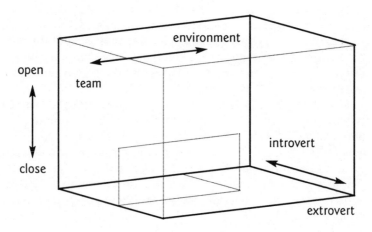

Figure 3.3 Behaviour in teams

Openers and closers

This pair of behaviour styles is concerned with the way people manipulate data and ideas. People who open things up are the data and idea gatherers. They will collect new evidence to enrich the knowledge base of the team. They will also seek to develop new patterns in the data that has been gathered. They tend to be the pioneers trying out new methods of working. Openers are comfortable with improvising and learning as they go. These are strong and positive benefits for any team. The downside is that these are the people who will always want one more piece of data before trying to make a decision. Good enough managers know that there is always a faster gun in the west; that there will be more useful data that could be collected, but the additional cost may far outweigh the additional benefit. The pioneering spirit will often manifest itself as a restlessness with the way things are being done now. Boredom is always a problem for people who like to open things up. The thirst for the new is what drives them on.

People who close things down are the decision-makers in teams. Or, to be more exact, the people who ensure that the team reaches a decision or a conclusion about the data it has. Closers are mindful of the need to complete the task, to bring things together. This can take the form of reaching an understanding about the data by drawing conclusions, summarizing where a discussion has been reached or proposing a solution. The closing instinct is a powerful one in us all. However, we all have different thresholds about where we are prepared to draw the line. I may settle for a big picture which gives a broad outline of the state of the world; you may want a line-by-line description. Closers often like to establish routine and bring order to the chaos of the data. For a task-driven team these are powerful benefits. A team filled with closers would be slow to adapt to changes in the world and might demonstrate a higher propensity to satisficing (see Chapter 6).

Focus on the team and focus on the environment

This pair of behaviour styles is concerned with the perspective of the individual: is their primary concern inwards towards the team or do they prefer a global view of the world?

Those who are focused on the team will be concerned to draw out the data that exists within the team and then create patterns

37

or understandings of that data. They will be concerned to establish and sustain the team's routines. The team's historian will fall into this category, recording present actions and recalling past actions. These are strong team players. However, a team which is entirely focused on itself will become isolated from the rest of the organization and will have a tendency to develop group think. They are also more likely to be convinced that their way of working is the best.

Those who are focused on the environment are sometimes called scanners. They will be able to bring to the team's attention changes in the outside world which may affect the team. Openers who are also strong scanners will seek out news and gossip and network widely. They will also act as the team's champion in the wider world, representing the team's performance. Closers who are scanners will often be the team's politicians carefully weighing how any decision taken will be greeted in the outside world. The team's empire builders will also be scanning the horizon for new opportunities for the team to expand its domain. A team full of scanners will have a very rich view of the world, but runs the obvious danger of failing to attend to the task at hand.

Introverts and extroverts

The final pair of behaviour styles contrasts where people derive their energy and inspiration: from themselves or from others? Are they introvert or extrovert? This does not refer to some shyness scale, introverts can be very bold people, but to the psychic compass that guides people's actions.

For an introvert this compass is held internally. They have to be true to themselves. These are the artists in the team, driven always to achieve the enormously high standard they have set for themselves. The result is often an astonishingly high degree of technical competence. Paradoxically, this can sometimes be combined with low confidence and self-esteem. The problem for the rest of the team is that introverts know when they are right and will be not budged. The flip side of the artist is the prima donna. Introverts are often poor at relationships with other people because, in the great scheme of things, the views of other people are not that important. Introverts can bring loyalty to the team and a sense of personal responsibility and commitment.

Extroverts are people-people. Their compass is provided by a wide range of relationships with other people. When you are trying to reach a decision, they will be the ones concerned that everyone is on board. Where an introvert will tend to be absolutist, a choice is black or white, right or wrong, an extrovert will see all sides of the questions and the choice will be a relative one between two shades of grey. Extroverts are the team players in the team, seeking to build consensus. The downside is that they are often uncomfortable with conflict and can find making a non-consensus decision very difficult. A team full of extroverts would talk a lot and could be more concerned with their own relationships than the needs of the task. Extroverts are to be found in the mainstream, following rather than leading fashion.

By now you will have worked out that all teams need a mix of all these behaviours in order to work effectively. For example, the team needs to be open to new data and new opportunities in the environment, but also needs to make decisions and progress towards their goal; it needs to sustain itself as a team and be aware of the wider environment; it needs people who will drive the team on and those who will look after each other. And so on.

As a manager you will need to strike a balance between:

- playing to people's strengths, otherwise everyone ends up doing things they are less good at and the performance of the team will suffer;
- the need to develop people and to give them new challenges to keep the job fresh and to develop their career;
- the requirement to achieve the task.

If you find that your team lacks, for example, any environmental scanners you can organize to compensate. You might ensure that each team meeting has an item on News from the World where team members share information or you might allocate responsibility to one team member to find out what is happening in neighbouring trusts or practices.

These three pairs of behaviour style give you three view points with which to understand the people in your team and how they relate to each other. If you can understand where people are coming from, managing them in the direction you want them to go becomes easier.

Jerry Rhodes' Thunks

Thunks have been developed by Jerry Rhodes out of work he originally began with Philips in the 1970s. This has now been extended by a continuing international research programme. Thunks is a language of thought. It is about the process of thought, how we think, rather than what we think.

Rhodes' research has identified three main approaches to the way we conceptualize our world. We do the following:

- Judge.
- Describe.
- Realize.

Rhodes attaches colours to each of these thinking styles: blue for judging, red for describing and green for realizing (Rhodes, 1988).

We use all three approaches in our thought. When we are Judging, our goal is to conclude what is right or true. When we are Describing, we are seeking to establish what is known to be true, what is or was. When we are Realizing, we are seeking to find something original, beyond what is already known, to explore what might be.

The precise mix of approaches we use will be partly set by the circumstances we find ourselves in. For example, diagnosis of a patient will find us mainly describing the symptoms and judging what they mean. The mix will also be influenced by our own personality. We all show biases towards thinking styles we feel more comfortable in.

Two things flow from this approach. First, the way individuals in the team tackle any task will vary according to their preferred thinking style. Imagine our team has three members: John who prefers judging, Deidre who prefers describing and Rasjid who prefers realizing. What will happen if we ask them individually to prepare a report on a new service? John's report may look at issues like: is this new service needed? What benefits and costs will it bring? Deidre's report may provide descriptions of other similar services we might use as a model. Rasjid's report may question the need for the service at all and come back with ideas about an entirely new approach to care. These are all valid points of view. The point is that they are different and that difference has sprung from the different ways the team members think about the world.

The second outcome of this approach is that it provides the team as a whole with a language for their work together. It provides an insight into why, for example, the three reports prepared by John, Deidre and Rasjid turned out so differently and gives a set of mental tools with which they can maximize the benefit from the differences in the team.

The Role of Patients and their Carers in the Team

When discussing the boundaries of care teams, sooner or later the central issue of patient and carer involvement comes up. Are they part of the team, and perhaps more importantly, should they be?

On one side of the argument is that with the increasing amount of health care being delivered in or close to home, it is inevitable that patients and their carers will play a larger role. If they are playing a larger role, and that is our expectation, then there should be a clearly defined role for them in our team. After all, they have more knowledge about their condition and the effectiveness of any treatment and the removal of health care from the power of arrogant professionals is to be welcomed. The case has been well made that the single factor contributing to the recovery of most patients is simple tender love and care. Carers are committed to their patient and, in some circumstances, be available for 24-hour care. Last, but by no means least, they require little or no payment.

Against this runs the counter-argument that patients and their families should not be exploited by a cash-strapped health service. And that although patients and their families have a general perception of the condition, they lack the specialist knowledge of clinicians and other professionals. They clearly lack objectivity and are concerned only with their own illness and not in the difficult balancing decisions that the provision of an equitable service demands.

Ethically it is clear that the defining principle must be that, as far as they are able, patients should be in control of their own lives and treatment. The reality is that some patients want that responsibility taken away from them. They want to be told what to do and they expect the diagnosis and treatment to be correct. Most will want to be involved and feel supported by staff taking the time to provide information about their condition and its treatment and explaining organizational procedures. Many general practices and hospitals provide patients with a general guide to their services and some have a patients' library containing information about diseases and treatments. This is all useful, but many patients and carers want to move beyond this. Being ill or watching over a loved one who is ill can be a very frightening experience. The sense of powerlessness only adds to the stress of the situation. The question for you as a manager is, can your team respond flexibly to these differing patient demands or are you providing a one size fits all service?

A report by the Carers National Association, 'Ignored and Invisible? Carers' Experience of the NHS', published in 1998, showed that in a sample of more than 3000 carers, less than half had been told about the type of care their loved one might need after discharge. While 70 per cent of respondents had been consulted about discharge arrangements, nearly a third of respondents felt that their comments and concerns had not been taken into account by staff arranging discharge. Only a quarter of the sample had been given a copy of the care plan. Almost 90 per cent of carers had not been given any advice or training in lifting and handling. More than half had suffered either an injury (usually to their back) or succumbed to a stress-related illness.

How Do Multi-disciplinary Teams Differ from Uni-disciplinary Teams?

The phases of team life that we have just looked at hold good for all sorts of teams. But this is a book specifically about managing multi-disciplinary teams, so what is it about multi-disciplinary teams that makes them different from uni-disciplinary teams? For me there are two main differences: one, a matter of philosophy, the other, of practicalities.

The whole point of multi-disciplinary teams is to bring together a range of different perspectives about the care of patients. This means that there is, at the beginning, no shared world view, no common understanding about the issues and symptoms which are of particular importance. Nor are there shared values about the form the treatment should take. It is your task as the manager to lead your team through their development so that they understand and respect the differences and those differences become a source of strength not a source of weakness. This is a theme you will need to return to from time to time.

We are an inter-disciplinary team working in a psychiatric intensive care unit. We work this way because we feel it minimizes the deleterious effects of any one treatment on other clinical problems and optimizes the eventual treatment of the entire range of clinical difficulties. With complex and multiple clinical issues, it is advantageous to coordinate the different facets of treatment. To the staff the label 'inter-disciplinary' implies that all members and disciplines on the team recognise the abilities, skills and critical contributions of each of the other disciplines. We often use the example that the lowest paid member of the team, the nursing assistant, is the person who actually has the best working knowledge of the level of functioning and the level of risk with an individual patient. The treatment team meet daily and attempt to reach a consensus on all major treatment issues. We maintain the norm of following the most conservative recommendation of the team members present in these daily treatment review meetings. Without occasional review and reminders of the model, there can be a tendency to revert to the more typical medical model in which the physician is the leader of the team with primary decision-making responsibility.

(Dr Robert A Zeiss, 1997)

On the practical side, the different power positions that people have in the system can be a major source of tension. This can of course be true within a uni-disciplinary team but a disagreement between, say, a consultant and an SHO working in the same

'firm' is of a different order than that between the same consultant and a nurse because of the different reporting hierarchies
and the historical baggage that goes with it.

Life Cycle of a Collaboration

In the same way that Tuckman identified a life cycle for teams,
so Joseph McCann and Barbara Gray (McCann and Gray, 1986)
have identified a life cycle for collaboration. They highlight three
main stages in the development of a collaboration (see Figure
3.4). These are:

- Legitimacy and recognition.
- Agreements on action.
- Allocate roles and responsibilities.

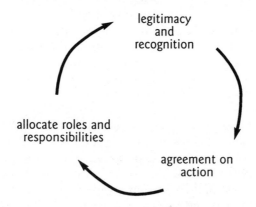

Figure 3.4 The collaboration life cycle

During the first phase there is a great deal of concern among the
collaborators about establishing the right to be a member of the
collaboration. And most crucially to have that right to participate recognized by others. This is similar to the forming stage in
the team theory. It is reflected in the concerns, particularly of
junior staff, to feel that they are proper members of the team.
Junior staff are often most interested in the way the decision is
taken rather than the actual decision itself. 'I want to feel I have

my views listened to and respected' was one typical comment from one of the focus groups I ran when researching this book.

The second phase that McCann and Gray identify is that of agreeing actions. Significantly they talk in terms of agreeing sufficiently for action to take place. This contains the hint that collaborative groups like multi-disciplinary teams have a habit of fixing on the lowest common denominator or the first thing they can agree on rather than pushing through the storming phase for a better solution. This phenomenon is called satisficing. I shall talk more about this and how to avoid it when I discuss goal setting in Chapter 6.

The final stage for McCann and Gray is the allocation of roles and responsibilities to achieve the task. They are adopting an optimistic and rational view of the process of collaboration: ie, roles and responsibilities will follow and be driven by the collaborators' goals. Sadly, for many collaborations the order is reversed with roles and responsibilities being used to set the agenda for the team's goals. This kind of jobsworthiness is particularly prevalent when individuals are defensive about their role and position. Then the important thing becomes maintaining my position as a nurse, doctor or whatever and the goals I want to see developed are those which allow me to do this. In other words, the service is being driven by the needs of the professionals rather than by the needs of the patient. This type of behaviour can surface at any time. One way of dealing with it is to cut it off at the start by promoting a professional attitude based on flexibility, trust and patient-centredness during the norming phase.

Pulling It Together

Analysing where your team is at the moment

There are a large number of techniques which are available to you to help you describe your team. There is a whole battery of psychometric tests which you can do. There also self-audit questionnaires like the Learning Styles Questionnaire. The Training and Personnel sections of your organization will be able to advise you on what is available.

Take a moment to reflect where your team is in relation to the life cycle of a team and the cycle of collaboration. The two life cycles of team and collaboration do not neatly dovetail with each other, but they do give you two ways of analysing where your team is currently. The best way to analyse where your team is to listen and observe.

- Listen carefully to what your team are saying to you and to each other. Are they talking about rules of behaviour (norming) or are they battling for air time (forming)?
- Watch the way they are working together. Is one person taking more of a lead than the others? Is there someone who looks as though they are about to say something but then keeps quiet? Is anyone else drawing the quiet ones into the discussion? Are roles defining goals or goals defining roles?
- Note what they are not saying to you and each other. Is the main concern about the way the team works together (norming, storming) or more focused on the achievement of the goals (performing)? Is there much praise and support going on among team members? Do the team members have a name for the team?

Below I set out a simple questionnaire you can use with your team members which addresses the key characteristics of the successful team we have identified in this chapter. There are no right and wrong answers to these questions. You might complete this questionnaire in a one-to-one with each of your team members or take time during one of your regular team meetings. Finally, you could set up a special meeting of your team. The important thing these questions will do is to get you and your team talking about the things that are important in a successful team. It is the discussion and the conclusions that you all reach which are important.

- Who do you think is currently in the team?
- What would you say the goals of this team are currently?
- What is your role in this team? What roles do you think other people play?
- Do we have the right mix of skills and knowledge in the team to achieve the goals that we have?
- Does the team have rules that it operates by, either formally or informally?
- What do you get out of being in this team?

These are very simple questions but they will give you a wealth of useful data. Don't expect the same answers from everyone. As Rhodes points out, everybody has a different perspective on the work. Don't be frightened to ask for fear of the answer you might get. Imagine the worst it can possibly be: no one knows who is in the team, what the goals are, what their role is, there are huge skills gaps, no team work of any description and no one is enjoying it. Now at least you know. Your job is to turn it round and the techniques and approaches in this book will help you do that. So don't be depressed by bad news. It is giving you a platform to build from. If you ask the same question in six months' time and still get a negative response that's the time to be worried!

What sort of team do you want?

As I tapped that heading into my computer the question: 'who are you?' came into my mind. Is it you the manager or you the team? I'll talk more about ownership in Chapter 5, but for now the message is a simple one: people are always more committed to targets which they have set themselves than ones that have been set for them. The goals of your team will probably be set by the organization or your boss. They will be the given targets that you will have to work with. But there is no reason why the other four success areas of clear roles, mix of skills and knowledge, good internal processes and personal benefit cannot be designed and evaluated by the whole team against the goals they have to achieve.

With small revisions, you can use the same set of questions you used to get a sense of where things are today.

- What should your role be in this team? What roles do you think other people should play?
- What mix of skills and knowledge in the team do we need to achieve the goals that we have? How can we get it?
- What rules (or norms) should the team have so that it functions smoothly?
- What do you want to get out of being in this team?

Hopefully, you will easily reach a consensus, although you may find some are easier to achieve than others. For example, there may be a reluctance to take on roles which are perceived as difficult. Agreements which were actually based on a fudge or incomplete information may come apart later on. Don't worry, building a team takes time and you will often have to revisit decisions and discussions. I'll talk more about this in the next chapter.

If you have this discussion with your team and you begin to make some agreements and consensus about how you will work together and who is going to do what, congratulate yourself and them. You have reached Square One, an achievement which is beyond a lot of work groups!

Conclusion

In this chapter we have reviewed the life cycles of teams and collaborations and looked at your changing role in managing these processes. Finally, remember at all times that teams move back and forth between the stages and that different parts of the team may be at different stages. This makes your job much more complicated, but also a lot more interesting.

As a manager you can make a real difference to the speed with which your team gels and to its overall effectiveness. In the following chapters we look at some techniques for making it happen.

Chapter 4

Leadership in Multi-disciplinary Teams

Introduction

The attraction of uni-disciplinary working in the NHS is tremendously powerful. The hurry scurry of the patient production line makes finding time to develop relationships and common views among staff difficult. And it is easy for people to slip back into uni-disciplinary habits that are deeply ingrained among staff and often supported by powerful organizational structures and cultures. At times, managing a multi-disciplinary team can feel like running up the down escalator.

The next two chapters look at leadership and management and how they can contribute to pulling multi-disciplinary teams together. This chapter looks at the following topics:

- why leadership is important;
- the differences between leadership and management;
- asks whether leaders are born or made;
- the myths of leadership;
- what leaders actually do.

Why is Leadership Important?

It is a truism to say that the world of work is undergoing constant change and the NHS is no different. For many people,

49

change is not something that comes easily into their lives. We have a need to feel grounded in our work. After our love, our labour is the most precious thing we can contribute to the world. Change will often pose a direct threat us. If I lose my job during a restructuring, I won't be able to pay my mortgage. Even if the all-important salary is not under direct threat, change which creates opportunities also leads to loss and displacement. All of this weaves together into a malaise that is haunting the British workplace. If a 'job for life' is a thing of the past, where does that leave someone with a vocation to work in health care? 'This is not the profession I joined' is a comment I hear often. The threat that people are feeling is very direct and personal.

People pick up very quickly if the sense of direction and energy that leadership should provide is missing. There is nothing worse when you are in a junior position without much power or status to feel that those who do have the power don't know what to do with it. Any direction is better than no direction is a conclusion that some have drawn. And there is some truth in it. It emphasizes clarity and decisiveness. It is also the approach which has got the Grand Old Duke of York a bad press down the years. He is still remembered in the nursery rhyme for marching his men to the top of the hill and then marching them down again. And the NHS is filled with the dust thrown up by the reverses in policy direction of the last few years. People who work in the caring professions are smart. Whichever leadership style you adopt, they will quickly work out if you know where you are going and whether they think it is a good direction to move in.

Imagine a Monday morning. You join ten people in a queue at a bus stop. According to a 1997 survey carried out by the Institute of Personnel and Development, only five of those people are looking forward to going to work. Four definitely don't want to have to go this job and one is not sure. Your job as a leader is to keep the five enthusiasts keen, swing the waverer and energize the discontented.

Leadership and Management

No single area of organizational behaviour has been more researched and debated than leadership and management. There are many who would argue that leadership and management are interchangeable terms. In ordinary conversation we do tend to swap back and forth between them.

Some commentators, such as Lickert (1969) and McGregor (1960), have argued that the object of those actions is more important than whether someone is described as a leader or manager. For them the right question to ask is whether the manager or leader is focused on the task to be achieved or the people who will achieve it. McGregor calls this Theory X or Theory Y, Lickert calls it job-centred or employee-centred. The point they are making is that we tend to be one or the other. Both can achieve results given the right context.

While this distinction is helpful, the blurring together of leadership and management does hide some important differences. They are different words with different meanings. Leadership is defined by the *Oxford English Dictionary* as giving guidance by going in front. Management is defined as being about conducting or controlling a business or enterprise. Immediately we begin to see that although the two are allied, what is, in fact, being described are different actions or states.

Furthermore, in the NHS the two terms tend to be used in different ways. Management is often associated with administrative tasks concerning the management of the budget. Leadership is often associated with activities like the clinical leadership of doctor or PAMs. The terms are not interchangeable or neutral.

Zaleznik (1977) has argued that these two roles could be distinguished as follows:

- Leaders – are active not reactive, shaping ideas not responding to them, and adopt a personal and active attitude towards goals. They are future-focused and develop expectations and desires about how the organization should develop.
- Managers – rationally assess the present situation; marshal resources; systematically select goals; design, organize, direct and control the work. They are concerned with performance and reward.

This is a helpful contrast, however, it again offers up an either/or choice. You can either be a leader or a manager. But we know that in different circumstances different actions are called for. For example, the response by an A&E team to a major road traffic accident calls for organization and order, not vision statements about the future. Yet the sudden bequest of a substantial donation from a grateful patient specifically for that same team opens up new horizons and possibilities for them by perhaps purchasing a piece of equipment or funding an innovative research project.

Integrating the two models into one gives us a richer map with which to understand our preferred style and the sort of response the present situation calls for (see Figure 4.1).

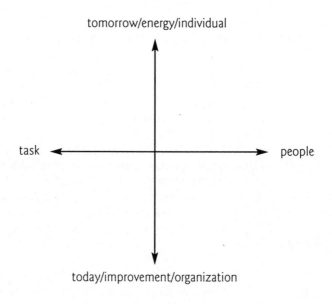

Figure 4.1 The leadership map

Four Types of Leadership Style

It is possible to identify different leadership styles in an organization. There are many variations, but I will focus on four:

- The superhero leader.
- The democratic leader.
- The bureaucratic leader.
- The reluctant leader.

The Superhero Leader – is a man, and it typically is a man, of action. In control of their environment, in complete command of the technical aspects of the job, bending nature to the force of their will. They are aloof from their staff, brooking no disagreement, thinking big thoughts, their eye on a distant horizon. There are many examples of the superhero leader from history: Napoleon, Alexander the Great, Karl Marx. Each surrounded by a cult of personality, each achieving staggering success which for them outweighed the human cost. Focused exclusively on their task and their destiny to remake their world in their own image, they would reside in the top left-hand quadrant of our model of leadership. It is a very prevelant and dominating leadership style in the health service and elsewhere.

The Democratic Leader – stands at the opposite extreme. They are focused on their people and their staff. They do not seek aggrandisement for themselves, just progress for their constituency. Their style is consensual and discursive. To the superhero leader, they are constantly being bogged down in the reactions of their staff to present circumstances. In their own eyes they are moving only as fast as their staff are able to move. The democratic leader does not seek to lead from the front but to act as a catalyst and advocate for their people. In historical terms, a good example of a democratic leader was Gandhi who, in spite of his fame and pivotal role in Indian independence, was never elected to any position either in the Congress Party or post-independence India. Gandhi's distinctive contribution was not the vision of an independent India, which had been discussed by nationalists for some time, but passive resistance – the method of achieving it. He would sit in the bottom right-hand quadrant of the leadership model, focused on people and moving forward from today towards the ultimate goal.

The Bureaucratic Leader – is the person who understands the organizational machine and how it can be made to work for their own ends. They are the people to be seen slipping down corridors, stitching deals together over the photocopier, making every use of organizational systems to provide them with control and power. They understand that the organization exists to deliver its objectives. A historical example would be Niccolò Machiavelli who ran the Florentine city-state for the Medici for 20 years. Machiavelli never did say the ends justify the means, but he did bring a pragmatic and cool order to the febrile world of late fifteenth-century Florence which was a bubbling cocktail as the heretical genius of Galileo rubbed shoulders with the inspiration of Michaelangelo and chancers like Amerigo Vespucci. Machiavelli would reside in the bottom left-hand quadrant of our model, focused on the practicalities of the task in hand.

The Reluctant Leader – there are many people who find themselves in leadership positions almost by chance. They had never really thought of themselves that way, but the job was advertised and someone cajoled them into applying. They never thought they'd get it, but what the hell, the money was good: let's go for it. And then suddenly they have been appointed and now what do they do? The reluctant leader can fit into any of the quadrants, but the historical example I will use was firmly in the top right-hand quadrant. One day she was working in a nursery, the next day Lady Diana Spencer found herself blinking in the flash of photographers who would dog her for the rest of her life. Her transformation from shy Di to world star is an extraordinary example of what can be achieved with courage and determination. While she never controlled the media, she became very adept at manipulating it to her vision of a people-centred, child-friendly world.

There are many examples of leadership in the NHS. The superhero leader is the consultant supreme in their own position. It is a leadership style that many others have imitated. The costs and limitations of the approach are now being increasingly exposed. The democratic leadership approach is a style which is often adopted by new managers anxious to take everyone with them, but it finds the hierarchical nature of the NHS a difficult environment to thrive in. The bureaucratic leader is to be found throughout the NHS and is now probably the dominant style. The management of the cash limit, bed occupancy, waiting lists, pre-scribing budgets and the shifting power deals needed to achieve them all test the bureaucratic leader to the hilt. Finally, the last few years have seen a sharp rise in the number of reluctant managers. Nurses, doctors and other professionals have found themselves thrust into management positions and are often struggling to reconcile their personal vocation of care with their new organizational roles and responsibilities.

Are Leaders Born or Are They Manufactured?

For years the study of leadership has been hung up on the search for a definitive leadership type. This is based on the assumption that somehow leaders have specific personality traits that we can at least copy. Even now the bookshop shelves are filled with books which identify the characteristics of successful people. The line of argument runs that if you do what successful people do, you will be successful yourself.

There are things that leaders say and do and ways that leaders act. It is important for you to begin to collect examples from wherever you can find them, so that you have an extensive range of approaches that you can use. Often leadership is simply a matter of finding the right words for the moment. At first you can feel a bit of fraud mouthing a stock answer, but as you grow more experienced and confident you will get better at finding the words and actions which are right for the situation and for you.

Role models are important. They show that something is pos-sible and not just a dream. Whether they are fact or fiction, they can provide us with blueprints to follow in certain situations. One day early in my management career I remember my boss telling me as he prepared for a particularly difficult meeting that he was going to go in and pretend to be Lee J Cobb in the film *Twelve Angry Men*. It would give him a fixed reference point dur-ing a challenging experience.

However, slavishly following one leadership style is rarely consistently successful. Successful leadership is more often a question of finding the right approach for the particular situation rather than the iron application of rules of behaviour and style. Those behaviours and style may be highly effective in one setting but counter-productive when applied somewhere else. A nurse used to working in the 'jump to it' style of a large teaching hospital may find that a leadership style appropriate to that setting will not work as well as in a small general practice in a small market town.

The Myths of Leadership

The first myth of leadership is the assumption that only people in senior positions can lead. Leadership can be shown by anyone in the team. Indeed, in the most effective teams the leadership role will swap back and forth between members.

In a multi-disciplinary team you will be working with people who have far greater technical knowledge than you. You need to have confidence in that expertise. Delegation of responsibility is a central part of leadership and management. People thrive on being given the opportunity to show what they can do. They want to do the right thing by their organization, colleagues and patients. If they have a clear sense of direction, they can take actions which are appropriate. Your job is to enable them to exercise their judgement.

The second great myth of leadership is that only charismatic people can do it. That somehow to be a leader you have to be able to march into a situation, stand on an upturned waste-paper basket and make an inspiring speech. For me, confidence is far more important than star quality. You need confidence in your own ability and confidence in the talents of your team. Confidence does not have to be of the shouting it from the rooftops variety, it can be quiet and everyday. Confidence is contagious. If you are confident, your team will become more confident.

Generally you will be making decisions based on partial information because you don't have time to wait for all the information or the information you need doesn't exist or is too difficult to access. There comes a point in every leader's life when they are making it up as they are going along. This is OK. I'll discuss later in this chapter using gut feeling and instinct and in Chapter 5 the technique of emergent planning. As you become more experienced so your confidence will grow.

Shortly after I was appointed to my first proper management job I had to go into a potentially difficult meeting with a partner organization. Two members of our staff had a huge row involving much verbal abuse on the premises of the partner organization. I had agreed beforehand with my operations manager that he would do most of the talking as he knew the detail of the case and the personalities involved. Our plan was to draw a line under the incident and to move on. As I walked through the door into the meeting a flash of terror passed through me: what was I doing there? what was I supposed to say? The briefing that my ops manager had given me had gone completely out of my head. I couldn't even remember the name of the employees involved in the incident. It was all going to go horribly wrong and be my fault. So I sat still, looked stern and serious, nodded a lot and after about 20 minutes said: 'So where do we go from here?' I later heard from a third party that our partner organization had been impressed with the way handled the meeting.

Being a Leader – How To Do It

There isn't a right or wrong way of leading. There are only better and worse ways of handling this situation with this group of people today. What you have to do is deceptively simple. You have to do the following:

- assess the people you are working with;
- clarify the direction you are supposed to be moving in;
- understand the specific task you have to complete;
- check the available resources;
- motivate and lead your staff in the achievement of the task by selecting from a wide array of techniques, all of which you are highly skilled in and feel confident in using.

It's all very simple: diagnosis, action, outcome. What this does not take into account is the noisy reality of life: that your team has two vacancies so everyone's rushed off their feet; that you have two, possibly contradictory, goals, to provide excellent services and save money; that you had a lousy night's sleep because of a sick child; that you don't spend every spare moment with your nose in the *Harvard Business Review* keeping track of the leading edge of management techniques; and that there are more patients hammering on the door. Nevertheless in the noisy reality of life a simple step-by-step approach is often the best way of approaching the task.

Diagnosis

Tuning in

Before you walk into the room and see that ring of expectant faces waiting for you to do something, take some time to think about your overall approach and sketch out a broad game plan. This may be as simple as starting by gathering more information and then further assessing the situation.

The following questions will help to tune you into the general situation.

- Are you clear how the task of your team fits into the big picture? Is anyone? Do people agree what the big picture is?
- How much time have you got?
- What resources can you call on? Who is in the team? What skills, experience and wisdom can you call on?
- What is your boss expecting of you?

Instinct and gut feeling

Much of the rest of this book is about giving you frameworks you can use to diagnose what is going on in front of you. These will help you analyse situations in a rational way. However, I would emphasize the importance of trusting your instincts, your gut feeling; of developing managerial nous.

We are usually most open to this when we first meet people or when we first go into an organization. You can sniff out when things aren't right or there is a real buzz about the place. Use your instincts to give you a working hypothesis and then check out with a more considered analysis whether you are right or not. Every now and again you will be spectacularly wrong.

People are a lot more complex and interesting than a snap judgement would suggest. Relying too much on gut feeling can blinker us to people's needs and make us deaf to what they are saying. So do balance it with time spent listening, watching and considering the evidence.

Action

Your style
How you tackle any situation will be partly determined by your own personal style. Try answering these questions, for example:

- are you the sort of person who can work with an outline sketch of what you are going to do and fill in the details as you go along? Or do you need to understand fully the whole picture so that you can handle anything that is thrown at you?
- which do you think is more important: building the relationships between you and the rest of the team or cracking on with the task?
- are you happier exploring new methods or following a proven formula?

None of these alternatives are right or wrong, but they will make a big difference to the way you work. Suppose, for example, we are given a new project to manage on patient discharge. My preferred style might be to start with the people in my new team and involve them in the development of an outline plan, trusting them to use their expertise and skill to fill in the gaps as we come to them. With a new team this will probably require a lot of time to be invested at the beginning to develop the trust, support and mutual understanding. I might feel this is time well spent because of the long-term benefits it will provide. In contrast, your preferred style might be to understand the details and piece the final outcome together like a jigsaw from lots of little pieces. To do this you might emphasize getting on with the job and getting people working in twos and threes on small parts of the problem rather than everyone figuring out how the whole system works and then how the pieces can be fitted together. As you can see, if you observed these two leadership approaches and the two teams using them, they would look and feel very different from each other even though the task they were working on was the same.

Let's take a different circumstance. You have just been appointed as the leader of an existing ward team. Let's look at a number of examples of how you might do this.

Suppose the team are well established with several long-standing members, performing effectively and with a distinctive culture. Now drop into that team a superhero leader who has a 'do it my way or else' approach to leadership. What will happen? The new leader may get results, shouting often works in the short term, but resentment will grow, morale will probably fall and the team may begin to break up, or worse, just sulk. Now try playing the same scenario with a democratic leader. This leader sits back, accepting that they are the new boy or girl in school and allows the team to lead and initiate him or her in their ways. Over time the leader becomes accepted and their authority grows because they are playing by the team's rules. You might wonder who is in charge, but does it matter if the team is performing?

Now let's look at the opposite extreme of a team which is completely dysfunctional – lacking shape, purpose and mutual respect. Now if the democratic leader lets the team set the tone, then the dysfunctional problems will just reinvent themselves in a slightly new form and no progress will take place until someone breaks the situation open. Now the superhero all-action style looks a better bet. Imposing a direction, cracking the whip and banging a few heads together and focusing on the task may well be what is required.

Adaptability

So to be a good leader you need to be adaptable; to vary your style according to the circumstances you find yourself in. Here we bump into a very characteristic human trait: the difference between what we say and what we do. I know that I need to adapt the way I work with people to the individuals I am working with and the situation we find ourselves in. I have been told this. I have read it in books. I have observed it when it has gone well and when it has gone badly. I have told other people this. And do I do it everywhere all of the time? Do I hell!

My defence is that I am better than I used to be. I used to tell people how adaptable my leadership style was. The reality was I led and managed every team and individual in every situation the same way. And I did it the way I would have liked to have managed and led. I was in effect not trying to manage them but managing myself. This is classic new manager behaviour: manage everyone as if they were you; recruit people into your team exactly like you. To be effective as a leader, you have to lead people in their own terms, get on their wavelength, speak their language. In this sense leadership is not about actions, it is about the reactions you get from your staff and whether those reactions take you where you want to go. Which takes us on to motivation.

Motivation

Most teams are somewhere between the two extremes and the right approach will be to mix some carrot and some stick. My own view is that roughly seven carrots to one stick is about right. Eric Caines, who achieved fame and some would say infamy as Director of Personnel for the NHS in the early 1990s, once said: 'It is not about beating people to death with the sticks, but pointing out that if they don't eat the carrots they will starve to death.' The point is that you need to have both sticks and carrots available in your tool box, the confidence to use both and the wisdom to know which one to pick in which particular set of circumstances.

It is sadly the case that people are more aware of their limitations than of their possibilities. There is all too often a poverty of aspiration. As a leader you need to follow John Harvey Jones' advice that people need a cuddle and a challenge. More broadly, people will only do what they believe, not what they have been told. So you need to find out what inspires them individually and collectively. Try asking the following three questions.

- What excites you about this job?
- What do you find boring or disheartening?
- If there was one thing you could fix about the way we work, what would it be?

Dangling carrots in front of people is the comfortable part of management. However, some people need to be pushed. Setting clear goals and not allowing people to slide away from achieving them is easier said than done. Using the disciplinary process is always the last port of call, but sometimes it can be the wake-up call that people need. A good formulation is to think about using the stick to get people's attention and the carrot to galvanize their commitment.

Motivation is as much about your commitment and enthusiasm for the task as it is any particular technique. If you are up for it, so will your team be. You'll have days when you feel stronger and days when you feel weaker. An awful lot about succeeding at work, at home, in relationships is just hanging in there and refusing to be beaten. Good enough management is being determined to do as well you can and trying to get better at it.

Outcomes

Achieving results is the objective of any team. As a leader you need to praise and reward people when they are successful. It is a scandal how often in the NHS good performance is just taken for granted, particularly from junior members of staff. Excellence often is standard, but that's no reason for not praising staff. Thanking staff is both good manners and good management.

Often the objective is merely a step along the road to the larger target. Maintaining enthusiasm and commitment is a challenge particularly when the larger goal, for example health gain, can feel so remote from everyday practice. You need to connect the small successes to the bigger picture.

Conclusion

The goal for the leader of a multi-disciplinary team is to develop a genuinely multi-disciplinary approach to care. The best way to do this is to focus on improvements that can be made to patient care. Putting the patient at the heart of the team's efforts diverts attention away from the differences that divide the disciplines in the team and taps into the basic commitment to health care that all staff in the NHS share.

Whether you decide to approach this goal through a task- or people-oriented approach or by focusing on the possibilities of tomorrow or the practicalities of today is a matter of personal choice and adapting to the circumstances you find yourself in.

Chapter 5

Managing
Multi-disciplinary Teams

Introduction

If leadership is the poetry of working with people, then management is the prose. Successful management is about mobilizing all the resources at your disposal and deploying them to care for patients.

In 1991 the Audit Commission published a report looking at how to make the best use of nursing resources in wards. They found that nurses at all levels often associated poor quality patient care with a lack of nursing time or resources. However, the Commission's researchers could find no systematic relationship between the resources available on the wards and the quality of patient care. They did find that successful, patient-centred wards were characterized by the ward manager's ability to release time for nurses to nurse patients by mobilizing all the ward's resources of people, time and equipment. Good management made the difference.

This chapter looks at managing teams and a number of techniques you can add to your tool-kit. It discusses four important elements in the management of any particular task and which you will have a particular responsibility for.

- Taking ownership of decisions.
- Meetings and how to run them better.
- Ensuring consistency in the delivery of services.
- Reviewing individual and collective performance.

However, the application of these themes and techniques needs to be placed in the very particular context of multi-disciplinary teams in the NHS. So we begin by looking at multiple lines of accountability.

Who's the Boss? Lines of Accountability

There are many things which make managing multi-disciplinary teams more complex than managing uni-disciplinary teams. In organizational and management terms, the most complicated factor is the multiple lines of accountability that individual staff members can have. You may have staff in your team who are accountable to you for some things, like the budget for example, but accountable to someone else for other things, for example, their clinical practice. Likewise, you may hold the professional accountability but not the managerial accountability. Or you may hold both accountabilities for some staff, but not for others.

This can be a complex tangle to unravel. It is important to be as clear as you can so that everyone, you, the staff and your colleagues are clear what the areas of accountability are and where the boundaries fall between them.

The problem is that in real life the boundaries between aspects of someone's work are often not as sharp as they appear on the organization chart. The link between clinical practice and the budget is clear but which way does and should the relationship flow? In these circumstances you may find yourself having to establish influence over someone who has the authority you lack. I will talk in more detail about techniques for doing this in Chapter 11.

Having more than one boss can also be confusing for the individual staff member. It also gives them the opportunity to play off one boss against another. This is the same trick children use on parents. Like wily parents, you need to be aware of it and to ensure good communication between you and your colleagues.

In some settings, like primary health care teams for example, the lines of communication between the bosses and their staff can become very stretched. It is worth investing the effort to make the connections. It helps to clarify the boundaries between you and avoids toes being trodden on unnecessarily.

Like many aspects of management and multi-disciplinary working, clarity is the aspiration but the picture remains stubbornly murky. Uncertainty can be very difficult, particularly when you don't know those who impact upon your team. Getting to know them brings clarity and will help to build the relationship so that you can jointly establish boundaries between your roles.

Ownership

Getting people to take ownership of decisions so that they actually are implemented is one of the key tasks of managers. The logistical pressures of getting people together often tempt you to cut your losses and make a decision yourself or to restrict the number of people involved in the planning process. Short cuts like this usually come unstuck fairly quickly.

It is a natural reaction that if I haven't been involved in a decision about how we are going to do the job, then my commitment to that decision will be weaker than those who were allowed to participate in it. This is particularly the case when other people are taking decisions about my job and the way I can do it. We have already discussed the importance of feeling that you are a full member of the team to the cohesion of the team.

Decisions also need to be owned by the organizational and professional hierarchies. In other words, they need to work upwards and sideways as well as downwards. Meetings are an important mechanism by which this can be achieved because they allow discussion to take place in real time, so saving time and effort.

Although it can take longer in the short term, sometimes a lot longer, the investment of getting all the right people in the room is usually rewarded in the long run. It means that you can ensure that the decision is clear, individual roles are clear and that people will actually deliver on their commitments.

In thinking about ownership, you will need to think about all the people who have a stake in a particular decision. Ideally, all these stakeholders should have the opportunity to participate in the planning process. This can involve a large number of people. For example, take the planning of discharge from a ward. People with a stake in this process will include:

- the patient;
- the patient's family;
- the patient's GP;
- the ward staff;
- the patient's consultant;
- the physiotherapist or OT;
- the community nursing team (in some instances);
- the porters;
- the providers of the transport (possibly the family, local taxi firm, or ambulance services);
- the staff at the nursing home (if appropriate).

You may be able to add to this list. The point is that the planned activity needs to work for all these people in this coalition of care. Somehow they need to have an opportunity to say what is important to them, to hear what is important to other people and to understand what is expected of them. It is tricky to strike the right balance between involvement and speed. Everyone working in the NHS is busy. You might look at combining some of the techniques I set out below to involve all the stakeholders in different ways.

Meetings

Why bother?

People in the NHS have a natural scepticism about meetings. They can go on forever and achieve very little. Vital people are often missing for all or some of the time. They can generate screeds of paper both before and after the event.

The interesting thing is that if you stop having formal meetings, people very quickly start complaining. They feel left out of decisions, they are unclear what decisions have been taken, they miss the information exchange and the contact with their colleagues. People actually don't mind meetings so long as they are well run.

There are a number of simple rules for good meetings. Good meetings should:

- start on time;
- have a specific purpose – an agenda;
- have the right people in the room;
- are to the point but not rushed;
- are chaired by someone;
- record and circulate action points.

This is not rocket science but everyday common sense. The thing that can make the difference is the quality of the chairing. The chair of the meeting needs to understand the importance of the balance between the needs of the task with the need to make and reaffirm relationships with other people.

> The one piece of advice I would give is to give time in each of your meetings for non-client business.
>
> (Consultant Clinical Psychologist)

It is through meetings that teams come into being. It is through meetings that teams build trust and the shared history of joint decisions and achievements. For the multi-disciplinary team, they are the workshop in which the shared understanding of the world is forged. In short, to be a better manager, run better meetings.

Techniques for running better meetings

There are many different techniques for running meetings more effectively. In the short space available here, I can only highlight some of them. For more information and help, check the titles in the Further Reading section or talk to your training department. I will look at just four:

- Future basing.
- Brainstorming.
- The Delphi Technique.
- Emergent planning.

Future basing

traditional

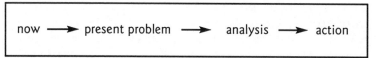

now ⟶ present problem ⟶ analysis ⟶ action

future-based

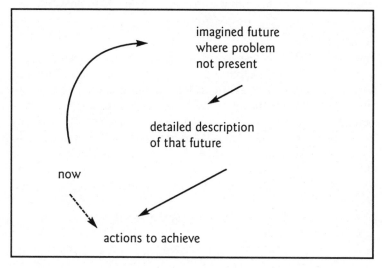

imagined future
where problem
not present

detailed description
of that future

now

actions to achieve

Figure 5.1 Approaches to problem solving

Traditionally, organizations have used problem-solving techniques which crank through an analysis of the current position, the reasons why things aren't working and then a technique that sets out to tackle them. However, recent research is suggesting that this is not the optimal way to plan. Research in the USA (Lippett, 1983) took two groups of managers and asked one to work in the traditional way by using a problem-solving technique. The second group were asked to imagine a future in which all the current problems had been solved. They were then asked to describe this world in detail. Finally, they were asked what steps they would need to take in order to bring this desired world into being. Comparing the results from the two groups showed that the group who used the problem-solving technique on the present situation became depressed by their predicament and showed little creativity or energy. By contrast the group who based themselves in the future (hence future basing) and worked back to the present were enthusiastic for the task, much more creative and, when the two groups came together to compare their results, came up with a better solution (see Figure 5.1).

It is a simple technique to use. Often the hardest part is convincing people that dreaming of a problem-free world is a legitimate and useful activity. It is because it gets people away from their normal way of thinking that it opens up new possibilities.

Brainstorming

Brainstorming is a technique which most people are familiar with. It is a very effective way of generating of lot of data and ideas in a very short time. It is also a technique that is generally not followed right through. Brainstorming is in fact a two-stage process. Stage one begins with the leader setting the theme or task. The participants then call out ideas and words that occur to them that are related to the theme or task. There is no discussion of any of the ideas at this point. The wilder and more creative the ideas the better. Even 'bad' ideas or 'silly' words can spark a better idea in someone's mind. This generates a long list of words and ideas. At this point most teams will get stuck into a discussion about those ideas in the normal way. And this is OK, if that is what you want. But particularly in large meetings the discussion can get stuck with one or two people or on one or two ideas.

Rather than discuss all of the ideas, take the time to filter what you have got. Filters are constraints or criteria which help you evaluate the ideas. They should be applicable to the specific issues you are discussing. Typical filters can include:

- cost – too high; within budget;
- time – can it be achieved within the deadline?;
- availability – the resources available to us;

- fit – is it in tune with our way of doing things, our image, our values?;
- patient impact – will it be positive or negative?;
- acceptability – will the idea be acceptable to senior management, funders, etc;
- practicality – is it doable? Do we have the skills?;
- developmental – will it help us to develop as individuals or as a team?

You can, of course, brainstorm what you think the filters should be. You may decide that some filters are essential requirements while others are only desirable. Once you have agreed your filters you can work your way through the list, removing those ideas that do not pass the various criteria you have set. Even with quite long lists you will quickly develop a short list of perhaps half a dozen. You might then move into discussing each of them in more detail before finally deciding.

Delphi Technique

The Delphi Technique is particularly useful for very large or dispersed teams. With the advent of e-mail it will become easier to organize. It requires one person to coordinate it. It requires participants to be prepared to listen to the views of their colleagues and works on the basis that all views are equally valid.

The Delphi Technique asks people's opinions in a series of rounds. The best way to explain it is to give an example. The Academy Award winners are selected using the Delphi Technique. The process begins with the Academy sending out a form to all its members asking them to nominate people and films under the various categories Best Picture, Best Director, and so on. These nominations are then collated centrally and the top five or six in each category are formally nominated. A second round of voting then takes place with each member being sent a second form listing the nominations in each category. Members make their selection, return it to the Academy, the votes are counted and 'The winner is...'.

The process is one of :

- gathering data from participants;
- organizing that data centrally and summarizing it;
- sending it back out to participants asking for further comment;

- gathering and summarizing those comments again centrally;
- sending it back out again.

You can have as many rounds as you want.

Emergent planning

It is a statement of the obvious that things move on in the health service: patients' conditions change, budgets change, staff move on. There is always an argument for, and often someone in the team who will put the case for, delaying a decision until more information is available. The problem is that there is no guarantee that additional information will actually answer the question, even if the right information is available. If you've only got partial information, then why not make a partial decision which is contingent on what happens next? There is a high probability that things will have moved on anyway. Emergent planning is just a clever way of describing this process of making small decisions which move you a bit closer to where you want to be. Let those decisions play out and then go from where you find yourself, even if isn't where you thought you'd be.

The idea of emergent planning allows some improvisation. Over-specifying and over-planning is usually a bad thing. As one health service manager has put it 'There is a real danger in trying to come up with the perfect strategy.' As policies change, organizations restructure, people change jobs, new balances of forces emerge. Emergent planning gives you some room for manoeuvre to cope with these changes. Emergent planning is not about abandoning yourself to your fate. Emergent planning works best where you have some good rules of thumb or general rules or an overriding goal. These act as anchors keeping you close to the things that are important, for example, involving patients as much as possible, looking for actions that simplify processes, and so on. Figure 5.2 shows an example where at each decision point there are three choices. The one that is chosen is the one that will take us closest to our goal.

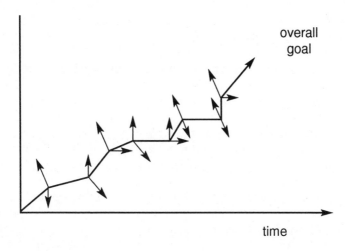

Figure 5.2 Emergent planning

Ensuring Consistent Delivery

Protocols and systems

Throughout the professions a profound and long-term change is taking place. We are steadily moving away from an expectation that professionals, whether they are doctors, nurses, teachers or social workers, will operate as independent practitioners guided by their professional expertise and ethos. In its place is coming a greater emphasis on systems and protocols: on precise and defined methods of working. This change is partly being driven by the desire to ensure consistency of approach towards all patients and partly to promote greater efficiency.

Protocols or standard operating procedures can be very useful ways of capturing and reproducing best practice. Their use has spread in recent years as management interest has focused on total quality and quality assurance. Quality assurance is a management approach which is about trying to prevent errors and failures before they happen rather than catching them at the end and throwing out the rejects.

A wide range of health care organizations are making increasing use of the results of clinical audit to inform the development of protocols which then allow all patients to receive the benefit

of the knowledge developed. They are also central to developments in skill mix. Training professionals and keeping their
knowledge updated is an expensive business. Is it the best use of
these expensive resources to have them doing important but
routine tasks, when a competent individual following a clear
protocol can perform the same task?

Systems and systems thinking can be really helpful in managing complex but regular parts of the work. It helps to keep you
on track with the routine and predictable elements of the work.
This means that you can afford to devote your main effort to the
unique aspects of any particular job.

The management of the complexities of winter pressures is a
good example of how systems and protocols can work. Most
hotels reckon they are fully stretched when average occupancy
is running at more than 85 per cent. They need some downtime
for routine maintenance and to allow for the surges that occur.
Most Trusts run bed occupancies of well over 90 per cent and
during the winter this can rise in some wards to well over 100
per cent. The increasing use of day surgery, shorter stays, rising
numbers of elderly people more prone to sickness during the
winter and the blocking of beds by people waiting for discharge
into nursing homes have all contributed to the increase in pressure on beds.

Bed managers now have an array of systems and intelligence
networks that they can deploy to keep the patients flowing
through the system. For example, assessment and discharge
wards provide gateways at either end of the patient's stay.
Computers can provide real-time information about the current
state of bed occupancies ward by ward. Good quality information from colleagues in public health and primary care about the
incidence of flu can give a guide to the severity of the winter flu
epidemic making predictions about likely future demand possible. Using protocols can streamline admission and discharge
while maintaining clinical standards.

Reviewing performance each year provides better intelligence
about when things need to happen and how long things usually
take. For example, Mondays are generally the worst day of the
week for admissions. The first Monday after the Christmas and
New Year holiday is particularly bad. Organizing this knowledge into systems and protocols means people know what is
expected of them and what they can expect from others. And so
gradually the systems get smarter.

The undoubted benefits of systems thinking and systems approaches mean that some people have gone overboard with them. The thinking goes along the lines of if one management control system is good, then ten management control systems must be great and 50 management control systems must be unbelievable. What happens is that we, and I include myself in this, become resentful and stop using them or do so only grudgingly. Which leads me to my rule of systems: they are usually only partially implemented. There are a number of reasons why this is so. It can be because:

- they threaten my autonomy to decide how I will do my job;
- I can see a better way of doing the job;
- it's more fun to cheat;
- they try to be too clever by half and are reliant on perfect operating conditions;
- nobody asked me what I thought;
- nobody explained to me how it was supposed to work;
- there was nothing in it for me.

So systems have their place, but for me they have to support rather than supplant the professionalism of you and your team members. People have to feel that they are running the system, not the other way around. The quid pro quo is that the systems should be used properly. Working with systems is like working with people, you have to build trust.

Good Starts and Poor Momentum

One of the characteristics of modern organizations is the quantity of change they have to cope with. As a workforce we have become very good at making starts on things as new initiatives and structures are put in place. But we seem to find it increasingly difficult to maintain the momentum once the initial burst of energy has passed.

There are a number of reasons for this. First, a new initiative, particularly when it has been developed and planned by the people who are going to implement it, often leads to a burst of enthusiasm and energy. There can be a real sense that this time it is going to be different. But then people change jobs, progress seems to be painfully slow, another organizational restructuring diverts attention away. The impetus is lost and the new project sinks back into the mush of ordinary working life.

All change takes a long time to bed itself into the fabric of an organization. Progress is often quick at the start because the relatively easily achievable targets are being accomplished. The more difficult, longer-term targets can prove insurmountable because not enough people are involved in trying to achieve them. All really serious organizational development requires a champion in a senior position who can mobilize the forces required to make it happen.

If you have experienced good starts but poor follow-through, another way to think about change is in terms of a series of small sprints rather than one long march. Instead of seeking one change that will lead to a 100 per cent improvement, try to find 100 changes that will each contribute a 1 per cent improvement. Small, short-term goals which are achievable build confidence and momentum and if they are all pointing in the same direction, for example, developing a patient-centred hospital, they will begin to feed off each other. To be motivated people need to feel the journey is worth while and that their individual step is achievable. It is a view of the strategic development of organizations and services that is based on incremental and evolutionary change rather than a big bang approach. For more on managing change, see the companion book in this series *Managing Change in the NHS* (Upton and Brooks, 1995).

Reviewing Performance

Reviewing performance or evaluation is a classic example where words and action diverge. Everyone talks about how important evaluation is, learning lessons from the past and applying them in the future. We are constantly assessing how we and other people are doing, but much of the time we are doing it in an informal way in chats over the photocopier or the coffee machine. As a manager it will be important for you to draw lessons for yourself, the team as a whole and for individual members.

Evaluation, like most things in management, combines technical and political aspects. There are two technical types of evaluation and two political types of evaluation.

The two technical types of evaluation are:

- Formative evaluations which are done as you are going along, for example, a weekly report on performance against specific targets like waiting lists.
- Summative evaluations which are done on the completion of a piece of work, for example, a report at the end of a pilot.

Information gathered from formative evaluations can be cycled back into immediate action. For example, your formative evaluation of your budgetary performance shows that you have overspent in the first two months of the year. You can then take action to ensure that you move back into balance by year end. Formative evaluations are going on all the time. They are the everyday stuff of managing performance. However, say the word evaluation to most people and they will think of summative evaluations. Summative evaluations can be particularly useful for transferring knowledge across organizations. Clinical audit is an example of a summative evaluation. A procedure is tested and adapted until it is thoroughly robust. It can then be formalized into a protocol and rolled out across a department or organization.

The two political types of evaluation are:

- Proving evaluations – where you are demonstrating to a third party, often your boss or purchaser, that you have done what you were supposedto, you have ticked the box.
- Improving evaluations – where you are seeking to learn and to improve your performance.

As you will appreciate, the way you handle and present information will be different depending on the purpose of the evaluation. If you are confident it is genuinely about improving performance, then you will be happier to share the disasters and cock-ups. If you think that someone will start marching around shouting and attaching blame because of a 'failure', you will gloss over the results to put the best spin on what happened. It is obvious that if this is done consistently, it breeds cynicism and the organization will operate in a miasma of misinformation.

A common mistake is thinking that all improving evaluations are good and all proving evaluations are bad. Proving evaluations have their uses. As a manager in the NHS you are responsible for considerable amounts of money and resources. As a taxpayer I want to know that my money is being well spent. There are plenty of other deserving services who could do with the money that you've got. Making you and your staff deliver against specific targets and requiring you to demonstrate that you are is simply holding you to account for the public funds you have stewardship of.

In addition, the NHS is a huge sprawling enterprise which is not in the control of any single person or agency. Nevertheless, it is possible to see that there are some things which it makes sense for everyone to do because it is good for the system as a whole, even though there isn't much direct benefit for them. Patient consultation was one example. In the early 1990s there were plenty of places where it was being done. However, there were also plenty of places where it was not happening. Requiring NHS organizations to carry out regular consultations does not guarantee the quality of those consultations nor that any notice will be taken of the outcome of those consultations, but it does at least guarantee that something will happen. Moreover, proving evaluations give legitimacy to local managers to pursue issues that they are interested in. For example, if you think consultation is important, the requirement on your organization to do something about it gives you the opportunity to volunteer to make it happen effectively.

Evaluating performance and you

Before I go on to describe some techniques for evaluation I need to ask you a question. When you ask a team member or the team as a whole 'how is it going?', do you think that they are hearing a question requiring a proving answer or an improving answer?

Evaluation and the team

I have already stressed the importance of clear goals to effective team working. You need to create opportunities to give feedback to the team on how they are doing in meeting those goals. There are innumerable ways you can do this, such as providing copies of weekly performance records at your regular meetings, and so on.

It can be a very useful exercise in team building to get the whole team to design its own performance scoreboard. To design a scoreboard will require agreement about what is critical to performance and so help to develop the common sense of purpose and ownership that underpin successful teams. You might think of it in terms of the critical life signs of your team: what would be the equivalents of a patient's blood pressure, heart rate and breathing. You might also think about signs which are not immediately measurable like skin colour and pupil dilation. If you decide to do this, stick with a small number of performance indicators; seven is usually a good maximum, five is better.

You will need to think carefully about what you want to record and how you will do it. The NHS is filled with data being collected for no apparent purpose. Beware in particular of collecting information which is merely interesting. Some teams only collect information to test joint hypotheses. For example, a primary health care team might test: 'we believe that spending three minutes at the start of our team meetings sharing news and information about the locality we all work in will improve our performance'. This could be done by a self-audit questionnaire before the start of the test and another one after three months.

In measuring performance there is one major caveat. Measuring anything changes the way people work. People throughout organizations are very adept at massaging data and its interpretation to produce the results they want. That is why is it so important to focus performance measurement only on those things which are critical to patient care and health gain.

One final point on evaluating team performance. Do make time to review the way the team works together, the extent to which people feel part of a team, the degree of trust and openness. This may produce some uncomfortable conversations and some storming, but frankness and honesty are two essential ingredients of effective teams.

Evaluation for the individual

There is no reason why the scoreboard idea cannot be used by individuals. The indicators may well be different, gathering more detailed information about the specific task. If, for exam-

ple, I have responsibility for finance in your team, my performance indicators might be: bills outstanding, invoices outstanding, cash position, speed of processing, and so on. The team as a
whole just needs to know: we're on budget, under budget, or
over budget.

Appraisal

Most health care organizations now have formal systems of
appraisal. These are reviews, usually on an annual basis, where
the staff member meets with their boss to look back over work
performance in each aspect of the job and then forward to the
coming period. It is an opportunity to review training and development needs and to talk about the direction the individual
wishes to move in. The idea is to keep off the nitty-gritty of
everyday detail, to step back and take a wider view. Your personnel department will be able to advise you on the particular
process your organization uses. Appraisals are not an excuse to
avoid talking to your team members during the rest of the year.
Everyone is busy with lots of calls on their time. But an essential
part of your job is to manage your staff and that means talking
with them all of the time about issues large and small.

A successful appraisal interview needs both parties to come
prepared with a list of the areas they wish to cover. Starting with
some good news is more likely to encourage people to think
about how they can do even better than starting with the bad
news. Handling the bad news is tricky. However, an interview is
more likely to lead to improved behaviour if such issues are handled non-judgementally and appraisees are encouraged to
assess themselves. The same neutral approach also makes it easier for the appraisee to talk about any gaps between what has
been expected of them and what has been achieved. Running
appraisal meetings well is not easy. Your personnel or HR
department will be able to offer advice.

A useful technique to use during an appraisal is the critical
incident analysis. Because of the domination of the blame culture and an expectation that management is about shouting at
people when things go wrong, there is an assumption that critical incident analysis can only be used when there has been a
problem. However, it can be used just as effectively when things
have gone well. Sometimes staff find it difficult to describe what

they do when they do their job well. This makes it more difficult for them to repeat the winning formula later.

Critical incident analysis works very simply by asking for a description of what happened. You then identify what the critical factors were that made the difference between success and failure, what specific actions were taken and what resulted and what might be done differently (or repeated) next time. It is, if you like, an action replay after the match where the player and the coach discuss how the goal was scored, conceded or missed and the changes that could be made to improve the result next time. I will talk more about critical incident approaches in Chapter 10, Developing Yourself and Your Team.

Dealing with poor performance

Discipline is usually the part of the job that managers find the most difficult. It is always hard to disentangle the personal feelings from the professional requirements of the job. The tangle of accountabilities we discussed at the beginning of this chapter just adds to the problem. It is always a big watershed in the life of a manager when after giving someone a rocket, their performance suddenly improves. It does work. Now your relationship has to become supportive, focusing on the good news. There are many reasons why people do not perform in jobs: they may not have the skills or confidence; they may have problems at home; they may be lazy; they may be bored; they may not be up to it. Some are forgivable, others are not. All require action.

> When I first came into the ward I realized I had a real problem with two of the staff. One was an experienced nurse who just wouldn't cooperate, the other was a much younger girl who was under the sway of the older one. I tried talking to them but they just took no notice, so in the end I invoked the disciplinary procedure. Personnel were really helpful. To be honest, I thought I would lose both of them. The younger one, who had really just been very silly, suddenly bucked her ideas up and knuckled down to become a really useful member of the team. It transpired the older one had got a lot of problems. She left the Trust soon after and started bank nursing. I'm not saying it was

> easy. It was a lot of hard work and stress, but the atmosphere now is so much better and we are working together as a proper team.
>
> (Ward Manager, Acute Trust)

Your first task with any individual is to ensure that they know what you expect of them. The clearer your expectation the better. If they fail to meet that expectation, you must take action or you are colluding in the problem. It may well be that encouragement or restructuring the task into smaller, more manageable bites will solve the problem. However, there are some staff who need to leave. This is not necessarily about sacking people, but facing the facts. If they are not motivated or are unhappy in this post, then you can help them find somewhere where they will be motivated and happy. There are plenty of people, myself included, who have been squeezed out of organizations and it was the best thing that could have happened.

If you find yourself in this situation, seek advice and help from your boss and personnel specialists. As a good manager you will ensure that the whole thing is done in an open and fair way and is in line with your human resource policies. There are times as a manager when you need to be brave.

Managing Upwards

Getting the best out of your boss is one of the most underrated management skills, but also one of the most valuable. A supportive boss who gives you the room to try things for yourself is a godsend. If you find yourself stuck with someone who lacks these sterling qualities, you need to come up with some plans for getting what you need.

Here are some useful tips and questions:

- Be clear what it is you are looking for: is it support? A sounding board? Or a referee to tell you when to pull back?
- What are the things that your boss needs from you?
- Where is the common ground?

You do not have to like someone to work with them, but it certainly helps. You certainly need to know someone to work effectively with them. And while you are spending this time thinking about how you will manage your boss, spare a thought for how your staff will be managing you. Just as your boss cannot achieve much without you, so you cannot achieve much without your staff.

Conclusion

Management is rarely about making clear-cut decisions based on definitive information. More often you will find yourself weighing the balance of probabilities and having to position yourself in the grey areas. In practical terms it is often about managing dilemmas, such as:

- When you need to gather information, do you go wide to develop the big picture or go deep to internalize the detail?
- Do you control what happens or delegate authority to others?
- Do you go for participation and involvement or go for speed?

The answer to all these dilemmas is: it depends. It depends on the situation you are in, how you got there, the expectations that your boss has of you, the expectations your staff have of you, your preferences and a dozen other factors. Good enough management is about making your best way through all of this. Being brave, trying things out, giving people their head and then learning from what happened is all part of the mix.

Chapter 6

Goals and Roles

Introduction

The research evidence is clear that the most effective teams, from an organizational standpoint, are those which have the clearest goals. Setting good goals which both energize and inspire team members and which are achievable is one of the key skills a manager has to develop, but it is also one of the most difficult. This is particularly so in multi-disciplinary teams where you are seeking to blend together diverse world views and value systems.

To help you achieve this, this chapter does the following:

- looks at two approaches to setting goals;
- discusses to whom the goals should and do belong;
- reviews the role of patients in setting goals;
- highlights the importance of staying flexible;
- looks at the problem of good starts but poor follow-through;
- concludes by looking at roles in teams.

Setting Goals – Possibilities and Practicalities

There are two starting points from which you can set off in pursuit of your goal. You can begin with the possibilities of the situation or start with the practicalities you have to work with.

These starting points represent two different philosophies of travel. The one is about allowing imagination and creativity to help you think outside the constraints of your present circumstances, the top half of the leadership model set out in Figure 4.1. The other is about moving from point to point and making the most of what you have got, the bottom half of the leadership model.

At various times you will need to emphasize one approach over the other and you will have your own preferred way of working. At all times you will need to find a balance between the demands of the two approaches. Whatever road you decide to travel, the destination is always the same – clarity of goal.

Possibilities

The possibilities of a situation can be explored by using the brainstorming technique we looked at in Chapter 5 or by getting people to use metaphors. A metaphor identifies an organization or service with a particular object or thing. Metaphors enable you to explore feelings and thoughts about a subject in a new way and to uncover surprising new insights. For example, you might ask all your team members to describe the NHS as an animal. I might say the NHS is like a school of whales. Large, intelligent creatures under threat of extinction who have a language of song which is excellent for communicating through the oceans but which ordinary human beings cannot understand. You might describe the NHS as a frog that hops from lily to lily without being able to settle and seems unsure whether it is happiest in the water or on the land. Each description builds up a sense of what, in this case, the NHS means to people. It does it in a way which if you just described the NHS in strictly practical terms, as so many hospitals and doctors and nurses and dentists and midwives, would not.

Using a metaphor like the NHS as an animal or getting people to draw a picture are all ways of making use of the right hemisphere of the brain. This is the part of the brain that, for most people, handles information in an intuitive holistic fashion. It is also the part of the brain we use less often. Much more dominant is the left hemisphere which deals with data in a rational and analytical way. We spend much of our working lives using the left side of our brain, particularly in the science-based world of the NHS. Making people consider subjects through the right brain opens them up and gets them thinking about their world in a different way outside of the normal routine.

Practicalities

This creativity needs to be balanced by pragmatism. The NHS generally does not have the resources to make great leaps forward. Progress is much more incremental and evolutionary. At the other end of the spectrum from dabbling in metaphor and drawing is the 1 Per Cent Game. The 1 Per Cent Game is really easy. You ask your staff what they would get rid of if the time they had available during the day was cut by 1 per cent. For an eight-hour day this is five minutes. Typically they will find something which is a waste of time which could be dispensed with. Then you ask what you would do if you had an extra 1 per cent, an extra five minutes available in their day. People never have trouble of thinking of something extra which would be valuable to do. At this point, you ask the question and what's stopping you doing that? Why not trade a poor five minutes with a more useful five minutes?

The 1 Per Cent Game is a good exercise for teams who are stuck and feel they have little control over their jobs. No matter how much pressure people are under, at the margins people can always take control of their work. This is particularly so when they can work together as a team. If everyone has got the same time-waster, but it is an organizational necessity that it is done, why not delegate it to one person and clear time in lots of other people's days? You can also play the 1 Per Cent Game with money: what would you cut if you had to lose 1 per cent from the budget? What extra would you do if you had an extra 1 per cent in the budget?

Whether you start your goal-setting from the possibilities or the practicalities, you will want to arrive at the same outcome: a clear set of goals for the team. There is a handy acronym which you can use to judge the quality of the outcome you arrive at. This is SMART. Your goals should be:

- specific in their scope;
- measurable in outputs;

- achievable with the resources you have available;
- relevant to the needs of your organization;
- timed to be delivered by a certain time.

This is a handy checklist, although it doesn't guarantee that you will arrive at the most effective goals.

Goal-setting Dangers

It is a statement of the obvious that people work differently in groups and teams than they do when they are on their own. Although we prize team work as a way of achieving more together than we can apart, there are occasions when teams achieve less than they would have if they had worked individually. Researchers have spent considerable time looking at the different behaviours of people working on their own and working in teams. There are three main dangers which you need to be aware of when setting goals in a group or team setting. These are:

- satisficing;
- group think;
- risky think.

Satisficing

Satisficing describes the situation where the group seizes on the first decision to which everyone concurs. In more everyday language, it is the lowest common denominator. There is a desire amongst all groups and teams to get along with each other and for people not to be seen to be difficult. Satisficing allows people to reach a consensus without having to challenge other people or be challenged by them. It marks an immaturity in the development of the team. They have deliberately avoided the storming phase in their development. A classic satisficing tactic is for everyone to agree that the blame for a failure by the team lies with someone outside the team.

When your team reaches an easy conclusion part of your job as a manager is to rattle the bars of the cage. Ask the following questions: is this the best we can do?; and have we really thought this one through? You might find an approach which gets the team using the right brain may waken some better ideas in them.

Group think

Group think is similar to satisficing in that it derives from a desire not to rock the boat. With group think, dissent within the team becomes muffled, so that people will go along with things even if they feel uncomfortable with them. It is a particular danger when there is a strong leader to the team. So if you are that type of person tread warily. You need dissent and disagreement within the team to get good quality decisions. And in extreme examples, group think can put people's lives at risk, for example, in a number of avoidable deaths of vulnerable patients like children or people suffering from psychiatric problems where individual professionals had concerns about the patient's safety but did not share their concerns because they did not want to be seen to be challenging their colleagues. Remember creativity is born out of conflict.

Paul was 15 months old when he died. He had lain in urine-soaked bedding and clothes for a considerable number of days. Photographs taken after his death showed burns over most of his body derived from urine staining, together with septicaemia with septic lesions at the ends of his fingers and toes. In addition, he was suffering from severe pneumonia. Paul's father was subsequently convicted of manslaughter and sentenced to seven years' imprisonment. His mother was also convicted on manslaughter and placed on probation for three years. The independent report into Paul's death found that primary care, secondary care, the probation service, police, social services and education had all been in contact with Paul's family for 15 years and concerns had been expressed by various professionals about his brothers and sisters during this period but no action had been taken. Throughout the period the various agencies and professionals had identified Paul and his brothers and sisters as being in need rather than at risk.

This common perception was not challenged by any of the dozens of professionals who came into contact with the family despite considerable evidence to the contrary. As a result of this common perception the report concluded that there were innumerable examples of poor or non-existent inter-agency and inter-disciplinary communication, and that 'there is no doubt in our minds that ... the quality of inter-agency co-operation fell short of what would now be regarded as essential.'

(Paul: Death through Neglect, Bridge Childcare Consultancy Service, 1995)

Risky think

Risky think is a concept that describes the way groups and teams will sometimes take more radical decisions than they would as individuals because they can shelter behind collective responsibility. In other words, the link between the decision and my personal responsibility for is broken. Risky think is a particular danger when there is a powerful, charismatic leader (who may or may not be the formal team leader) who argues powerfully for one course of action. The team may go along with it because to oppose it is apparently to place oneself in an isolated position. It's the same sort of process you might see in a school playground where kids dare each other to let down the head teacher's tyres and anybody who opposes the idea is taunted as chicken.

Whose Goals?

So far I have been working with the assumption that it is possible to develop a single set of goals and that there are no conflicts present. However, many multi-disciplinary teams bring together professions and staff riven with incentive and goal conflict. This can express itself in the following ways:

- goal conflict;
- conflict between staff;
- conflict with patients.

Goal conflict

Teams may be expected to produce high quality results while at the same time producing efficiency savings. The tensions between these two goals have become heightened over the years as the demands of the efficiency savings require ever deeper cuts in the fabric of the service. This can set up very sharp ethical dilemmas for staff and contribute to a sense of dissatisfaction and stress.

Conflict between staff

Differences between staff may also be present. These differences can also stem from differing personal agendas and from conflicts between professional paradigms. A paradigm is a system of thought which helps to define a body of professional thought. These paradigms are deeply engrained in professionals by their training, the culture of their professions and their continuing education. They are deeply felt and stir strong emotions. To take a simple example: if a doctor is simply concerned with the presenting medical condition they may find themselves in conflict with a social worker who is concerned with broader social causes of disease. To all of these conflicts can be added simple personality clashes. The initial task for a manager faced with this sort of conflict is to understand what sort of conflict they are seeing. Is this a clash between personalities or paradigms?

These sorts of conflicts can create a difficult environment for you to work in. There is a limit to the extent to which you can control these conflicts. It may well be the best you can do is to ameliorate them. Often the best way is to acknowledge they exist and to restate again your commitment to multi-disciplinary working and the development of patient-centred services. Managing in the NHS is a tough job and you will have good days and bad days. Take comfort from the knowledge that you are not alone. All over the NHS there are people beavering away.

Good enough managers know they will have bad days. They also know that unless they believe in themselves there is no hope of progress.

Conflict with patients

Patients will often argue for more resources for their particular condition while clinical staff have to take a broader view of meeting patients' needs from a limited pot of money. The almost automatic opposition of patients to the closure of hospitals and opening hours often cuts against the most efficient use of resources. One of the great mismatches in the NHS is between the professional groups driven by the desire to provide high quality services and the patients' desire for an accessible service. Sometimes the two are irreconcilable.

Role of Patients in Setting and Evaluating Goals

Setting goals

When you are setting your goals, you need to think how you can involve patients in their development. You can make use of a wide range of quantitative and qualitative surveying techniques or actively bring patients into the planning process. Some of the most successful planning activities have used children working in close harmony with architects and staff on the design of new children's facilities, for example the new children's hospital in Derby. If it works with kids, why shouldn't adults get to have a go?

A patient-centred service starts from discussing with patients what their needs are. Often when you compare the things that staff think are important with what patients say are important, two very different pictures emerge. Staff are usually most concerned with technical questions of quality. Patients take this as given. They trust their clinicians to do the best for them. Their expressed concerns often focus on aspects like access to treatment and information about their condition.

When setting your team's goals, a useful rule of thumb is to write them in patient-friendly language. A patient-centred service needs to be able to communicate with and listen to patients. Starting by setting your team's goals in terms your patients can understand sets the right tone from the beginning.

Evaluating goals

Often the most useful feedback you will get will come from patients themselves. A lot of organizations now regularly get patients to complete feedback sheets asking for comments about services. This can be done on a continuing basis or a series of snapshots at regular intervals. In seeking feedback from patients it is best to make use of a variety of channels. Some people will say things on paper which they won't say face to face. Others, perhaps people whose first language is not English or who are visually impaired, will find verbal feedback easier. Some will only tell you nice things because they don't want to get anyone in trouble. Some will complain about anything and everything.

When designing your feedback try to gather both quantitative and qualitative information. You can get quantitative information by asking a question and then providing a multiple choice answer. For example, how would you rate the approachability of staff? Excellent, good, OK, poor. This type of question will give you a score. You can set targets for these scores and monitor how they vary over time. Qualitative questions are the sort that ask for open comments about the service. Often the simplest are the best. For example, what was the best thing about your stay? What was the worst thing about your stay? You can collate the answers you get and look for the patterns in them. They will usually help you interpret the quantitative scores. For example, if you score well on the approachability of your staff, then everyone deserves some praise. If the porters are particularly identified in the qualitative answers, then you can particularly highlight their contribution. I usually add a catch-all question at the end like: is there anything else you would like to say? Most people leave it blank but it sometimes reveals something really informative.

The other useful source of feedback from patients is complaints. These are often highly informative. Make a point of collating them every six months or so and see what pattern emerges. Are they about breakdowns in communication, attitude of staff or things that are out of your control like cancelled operations because of shortage of beds?

Staying Flexible – The Importance of Plan B

There is an old joke: if you want to make God laugh, tell Him your plans. And there is another acronym to put alongside SMART: OBE – overtaken by events. Things do move on and can do so quite suddenly. It is not unknown for managers of multi-disciplinary teams to come into work and find that 20 per cent has been removed from their budget overnight. If you find yourself in this situation, you will be presented with a choice about what you do and it is a choice of options that does not need to be held back for catastrophic news. It is an approach called zero-based budgeting.

Zero-based budgeting starts from the premise of a blank piece of paper. Instead of beginning with the services you have at the moment, with the present level of staffing and the buildings and other resources presently available to you and then looking for a way of trimming a few percentage, you begin from first principles. Using zero-based budgeting you first establish the core elements of the service that you must provide and then work out how you could deploy the money available to do it. It can often lead to a radical rethink about roles and relationships within the team. Do we need two different types of post to provide these two similar services or can we combine them into one multi-skilled role? What happens if we organize people by function and skill rather than by locality? If we start from patient needs, what would our ideal skill mix be? And so on.

A Community Trust was informed by its health authority in March that there would be a 20 per cent cut in children's community services in the new financial year beginning in April. Most of the posts concerned were linked to GPs or schools. Rather than just cut 20 per cent across the board, they decided to take a more radical approach. They brought together consultants, paediatricians and health visitors to look at what the risks to children were. Having reached a consensus on the risk assessment, they were able to agree to stop doing all the low-risk work and provide for the medium- and high-risk work in an integrated way. New merged roles combining elements of the old health visiting and schools' nurse role were developed. An organization and personal development programme was initiated to facilitate the change and the whole programme was continually evaluated as it progressed. There was a common understanding that they had not worked out all of the details at the beginning and that the plan would need to be adapted as they went along.

Zero-based budgeting can be very threatening to the staff involved. Suddenly the whole history and value of the service they have provided to the best of their ability are being undermined. Their jobs and professional roles are thrown up into the air. The relationships which have been developed are disrupted. All of this means that a zero-based budgetary approach needs to be handled with care and sensitivity and it is not something to start lightly. Nevertheless, it has its place in the effective manager's briefcase because it enables a completely fresh look at the service that is being provided, unencumbered by the baggage of the past.

Roles Within Teams

For many multi-disciplinary teams, their goals are handed down from on high. The organization decrees that bed occupancy will be 95 per cent, the budget will be delivered +/-1 per cent of target, there will be a visit to every child within the first eight weeks of life, and so on. In terms of the model of multi-disciplinary working I set out in Chapter 1, the organizational dimension is driving the process.

The cultural dimension of the model appears in the goal-setting process in two ways. First, people will often define their goals in terms of what they can do and what they can do is often what they perceive their role to be. The argument becomes circular. For example, imagine I am a health visitor and that my approach to my work is as follows: 'I have been trained to visit young children, to monitor and support their development therefore my goal is to visit children and monitor and support their development.' My goals are being defined in terms of what I think my role is. Now contrast that with this approach: 'I am a health visitor. The children and families in my patch have the following needs. I have been trained and have a set of skills. My colleagues in the primary health care team have complementary but different knowledge and expertise. Looking at the needs of the children in our patch, we can blend our skills together in this way to meet those needs. This means, perhaps, that I will monitor children less often, say every nine months rather than every six, and use the time I have gained to do health education work with families at the local community centre.' Now my goals are being set in the context of the whole team and the needs of the patients we serve and my role is being derived from that larger goal.

This is an example of a true skill mix approach. Starting from the needs of patients and the talents available to serve them. Sadly, a lot of the work done in multi-disciplinary teams is, in the words of one Director of Nursing, 'based on habit not on need'.

The second way that the cultural dimension can impact on goal setting is through the setting of explicit multi-disciplinary goals. Multi-disciplinary working is not a natural style for many people. Setting goals that promote the multi-disciplinary process will help to get people into the multi-disciplinary habit.

Just as the cultural dimension of goal setting tends to be ignored in goal setting, so does the inter-personal. Setting specific goals in the team context for each individual can help to clarify people's individual contribution to the team. Another way to approach this is to review each of your team's goals and then ask, what is in this for the individuals in the team? If there is little or nothing in it for the individual, you will be failing to meet the fifth of the characteristics of successful teams I set out in Chapter 2.

With the goals set it becomes possible to work out the contribution of individual team members. This will emerge from the allocation of tasks. As team manager you should be playing particularly close attention at this stage. You will need to decide whether you allow the team to organize amongst themselves who does what, whether you do it for them or there is some mix of the two. There is a lot to said for standing back and allowing the team to organize themselves. A volunteer is always more committed than someone who has been instructed to carry out a task. Your role may be to encourage people before the meeting to volunteer and then supporting them when they do.

The roles taken on by team members will be shaped by three factors:

- What they are capable of doing.
- What they are expected to do.
- What they are allowed to do.

Capabilities

People in teams will quickly begin to fall into a pattern of who does what. Some people will always take on writing jobs, others will make contact with people outside the team, and so on. As team manager you need to ensure that you are not overly dependent on one person always being there to do something. There should always be an element in your team development of looking at multi-skilling and broadening people's range of skills and experience. Weighing against that will be the need to avoid the danger of playing away from your strengths. Doing something other than what you are used to and do well can become a fetish and people end up feeling frustrated.

Expectations

We very quickly come to expect people to take on some roles. If I always have done the reports, then I always do the reports. I may have only agreed to do it the first time because no one else wanted to do it and now I am resentful because it takes a lot of time and no one ever thanks me for it. Be aware of mismatches in expectation of roles. I may expect you to tell someone of our decision because I know you will see them. You may not tell them because I didn't specifically ask you to. This type of mis-communication and mismatch of expectation often lies at the heart of personal conflicts. Some senior staff are not prepared to 'work for' a junior member of staff. Others are happy to do it as they see it provides an opportunity to develop staff.

Allowed to do

Roles in the NHS are constrained by legal requirements. Clinicians have to exercise their professional skills with due care and diligence. So, for example, a GP is under a legal duty not to offer treatment to a patient that is beyond their experience or expertise. They have to refer that patient to a consultant.

Roles can also be constrained by hierarchy. A senior consultant in a teaching hospital may not be prepared to take a message from a junior member of staff, particularly if they are not a doctor. Some jobs need to be done by someone with the right job title rather than just the right skills.

Shifting Roles in Teams

The real point about roles in your team is that they can be fluid. In a high performance team roles get passed back and forth, for example, leadership will shift from person to person as the circumstances demand.

As manager you will have a view about how you would like the team to run, as will the staff in your team. People will naturally fall into relationships with each other and boundaries and expectations will develop. As the team manager it is your job to sense any of the frictions that these relationships and boundaries are causing. If you suspect there is a problem, don't just act. Instead, find an opportunity to have a quiet word with those involved and see how they are feeling about it. Don't be frightened to open out these tensions. If your team is going to develop, then its members need to be able to have adult conversations with each other. But people do have feelings and the last thing you want is someone in a sulk, so handle it sensitively. Naturally the secret of this will be communication, which is the topic we move onto next.

Conclusion

This chapter has looked at the core task for managers, that of setting clear goals. It is worth re-emphasizing that from the point of view of the organization, and as manager that must be a primary concern of yours, clear goals are the single most important element in creating effective multi-disciplinary teams.

Chapter 7

Communication in Multi-disciplinary Teams

Introduction

Communication is the bread and butter of team work. If we cannot communicate with each other, we cannot work effectively as a team. It is also the area which most multi-disciplinary teams say they have most difficulty with. Even problems which stem from other areas, for example, lack of clarity about goals, are often attributed to failures of communication. Usually the quickest way to improve team working is to work on communication.

This chapter identifies some of the main reasons communication can go awry in a multi-disciplinary team and some of the actions you can take to improve matters. Good communication is based on a mix of techniques. Some of these are to do with transmission which push messages out effectively and some are about attentive listening that pulls information and ideas in. In particular, this chapter looks at the following points:

- why communication is important;
- how people communicate with each other;
- making your communication work better.

Why Is Communication Important?

When I first go into an organization I always have to look for evidence of my Iron Law of Communication. This states that senior managers always think they communicate very effectively with staff and staff always think that senior managers' communication with them is terrible. Sadly, on many occasions I find evidence in support of the Iron Law. There are a number of reasons why this is the case.

There are some organizations which still do not think that their staff need to know what is going on and actively seek to control the information that goes out. Fortunately, there are considerably fewer of them now in the NHS. However, even in organizations that devote great effort to communicating with staff I still find support for the Iron Law. Often this is because senior management see communication as a one-way process: we inform them about what's going on, while staff, seeking to establish the respect and status we discussed in Chapter 2 on teams, want to say things to management. There is a classic mismatch of expectation and desires. Senior management think communication is about talking to staff. Staff think it needs to be about listening and in particular listening to them.

> Q: What advice would you give to a newly appointed manager of a multi-disciplinary team?
>
> A: Listen to your staff.
>
> (Paediatric Registrar, Acute Trust)

Sometimes management assume that because they have told their staff something once they have heard it. However, the message needs to be repeated several times for it to get through – a message I will be repeating several times in this chapter. These anecdotal experiences are supported by the research evidence. Indeed, the biggest organizational development initiative of the last decade, Investors in People, is a direct response to this problem.

If organizations find it difficult to communicate effectively with their staff, they are usually worse when it comes to communicating with patients. Again a great deal of effort has gone into trying to improve the communication skills of individual practitioners and organizations. But much work remains to be done. Partly this is about poorly constructed sentences, but even well-written sentences which use NHS-speak are not comprehensible to patients.

A survey by North West Anglia Health Authority showed that 36 per cent of respondents thought that primary care meant life-saving services in the NHS, a further 18 per cent thought it meant services for children under 11. Similarly, 51 per cent thought that secondary care meant less urgent NHS services and only 27 per cent identified it as hospital services. Some 66 per cent did not know what CPN stood for and 55 per cent did not know what triage meant or thought it meant treating people at home not in hospital.

It is your job to ensure that your team communicates effectively with each other, with other colleagues and with patients. If your team doesn't communicate effectively, how are you going to make the most of the knowledge and expertise that they have? Why should patients be kept in the dark about their treatment and their health service because we don't take the trouble to speak English?

How Do People Communicate?

Language sub-sets

It is the nature of specialization that specialist languages are used. This is partly the result of the need to invent new words to describe new phenomena as we discover them. Putting names to things is the very stuff of learning. The words describe concepts or lumps of knowledge. By using a new specialist language we develop a shorthand which speeds up conversations and means that we can manipulate more data and that helps to push our knowledge even further. However, my specialist language is your jargon. It also separates the initiates from the rest. When we train to become a professional we will quickly start to use the language of our trade in order to demonstrate to ourselves and our colleagues that I am a nurse or a doctor or a manager and therefore you should treat me as such. Using the right language is the gateway into the group.

In health and social care there are a multiplicity of specialists and hence a multiplicity of languages. Patrick Pietroni (Leathard, 1994) has identified 11 language sub-sets operating in health and social care.

- Medical, molecular, material.
- Psychological, psychosomatic, psychoanalytic.
- Social, cultural, epidemiological.
- Anthropology, ethology, ethnology.
- Symbolic, metaphorical, archetypal.
- Natural, energetic, spiritual.
- Prevention, promotion, education.
- Eenvironmental, ecological, planetary.
- Legal, moral, ethical.
- Research, evaluation, audit.
- Economic, administrative, political.

Pietroni argues that any one practitioner may be fluent in two or three of these language sub-sets, but they will not be fluent in all. Indeed, the values that underpin these sub-sets can be in conflict with one another. For example, by definition, a hard-line materialist will deny any spiritual dimension to care.

It is possible to argue with Pietroni's analysis. The language sub-sets can run into each other, there may be others that you can think of, but his general point is well made. Language, the very thing that should be bringing us together, is one of the things that holds us apart.

This multiplicity of sub-language has two consequences. First, successfully drawing your multi-disciplinary team together will require your team members to work in several language sub-sets at once. And, second, a practitioner reflecting on their practice will also need to reflect on the language sub-set they are working within. Thus, a doctor working with chronic rheumatoid arthritis may reflect only within the medical, molecular, material sub-set and search for another drug because they lack knowledge to consider approaches from within another language sub-set.

Frameworks of language

Pietroni's list takes account of the technical divisions of language, but there is a further layer that needs to be unpeeled. Individuals operate from within their own perspective or model of the world. Communication is only as effective as the response it elicits. In short, it is not what you say that matters, it is what the listener hears, feels or sees that causes the message to pass between you.

Irrespective of the technical language we speak, we each have a preferred way of processing and communicating information. These are shown in Figure 7.1:

- visual;
- aural;
- kinetic.

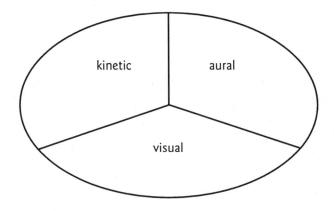

Figure 7.1 The frameworks of language

When we are in visual mode, we see the idea, get a picture in our mind, focus onto something, imagine an outcome. In aural mode, we hear the message, we tune into what is being said, or an idea rings bells for us. In kinetic mode, we feel our way towards a conclusion, we get a grip on a situation, we handle a difficult phone call, my gesture touches you.

None of these approaches to understanding and communication is wrong, but they are all different and each of us has a preferred mode. For example, I tend to spend most of my time in visual or kinetic modes, I don't use the aural much.

The best communication takes place when the communicator uses the language of the communicatee's world, so that if you are trying to get something across to me your best bet will be to use a mode you know I am more comfortable with. So, for me, you should paint me a picture or give me something I can get hold of. If you try to make me hear something the message may get through but I will have to work harder to assimilate it and you should be trying to make it as easy for me as you can. Unfortunately, most managers try to communicate with their staff in the same way most Brits communicate abroad. We assume the locals can speak English. If they don't understand, we repeat what we have said more slowly and if that doesn't work, we shout. If we still cannot get through, we will blame them for not speaking our language. Varying the modes of language you use will make it easier for different people to pick up on what you are trying to get across.

Plot lines

Humans are pattern-forming animals. It is one of the great strengths of our species and has been a powerful motor in evolution. Our experience of the power of making patterns is such that even where no pattern actually exists we will infer one and then act as if it is the case. This is true in the way we explain to each other what's going on in our organization.

Organizations are dramatic places filled with characters and events. Things are always happening. People get fired, promoted, blamed. They have affairs, cook the books, rescue situations. We explain these events to each other by telling each other stories round the coffee machine and across our desks: 'have you heard what's been going on the fifth floor today?'

Some of these stories are speculation, some are malicious, most have some hint of truth to them. We listen and evaluate these stories: do they seem plausible, do they fit with that we know? We repeat them, with or without embellishments. And all the time we are trying to anticipate what is going to happen next. How will this affect our department, my job, your future? In this sense we are all plot makers; dramatists.

A plot is the dramatic logic of a drama. It gives a shape to the events so that they reach a resolution. Successful story tellers know that, although humans have been telling each other stories since we acquired language, there are actually very few basic plots. Arguments vary about how many basic plots there are. Stephen Downing (1997) has suggested in organizations there are four basic plots:

- romance;
- tragedy;
- melodrama;
- irony.

All of these plot types are rooted in feelings. Each moves the story on, but their logic constrains the ways in which that story can develop: a romance will turn out differently to a tragedy. Let us consider the different plot types:

- The Quest – a progressive hero-adventurer challenges the status quo or conventional wisdom, experiences setbacks, but ultimately succeeds. Most romances follow this formula.
- The Downfall – a hero is pitched from success to danger and humiliation, primarily as a result of fate or external events. The classical tragic formula.
- The Contest – a polarized struggle between two heroes characterized as vice and virtue, or good and evil often over a third party which leads to a climatic battle in which the opposition is defeated. The melodrama or soap formula.
- The Scam – a hero is exposed as incompetent, corrupt or a fool; apparently heroic actions are reinterpreted as a scam to fleece others. The ironic or feet of clay formula.

It is easy to put organizational examples to each of these four main plot lines. Thus most mission statements cast the organization as hero on a quest. In this plot line, setbacks are an integral part of the successful outcome not a sign of failure. Individuals involved in organizational change often cast themselves in a tragedy. Most notably professionals whose professional autonomy is being challenged by management seeking to impose financial or other constraints. For agencies or individuals working in collaborative settings, the contest is a powerful plot line. The contest between the social and medical model of care for users and patients is one example, turf battles between powerful personalities is another. The scam is a powerful plot line often used by tabloid newspapers after they have built a hero up, they can knock them down again.

Imagine an organization that has undergone a number of changes at the senior level over the recent past but whose position is still regarded by staff as weak. A new chief executive joins and announces that the organization will go for a major quality award (organization as hero on a quest). There is scepticism amongst staff about whether this 'latest management fad' will make any difference (the scam plot line). This scepticism is heightened when it becomes clear that previously autonomous technical staff will have to become more corporate in their actions than in the past (a tragedy for the individuals who had previously seen themselves as heroes driving the company). Support staff hearing both the official version of events (the quest) and the griping of the technical staff (the downfall) may interpret the story as melodrama: who will win out this time? And so on.

Working life is not a play or cinema script. It does not come to an end at the end of episode. Characters do not live happily ever after. It is therefore possible to reinvent the story with a new plot line as new events happen. A good example is the way a tabloid newspaper may set someone up initially as a hero, but then reinvent the story as a scam – our hero actually has feet of clay.

Research shows that when organizations undergo periods of major change the level of gossip or talk within the organization increases dramatically. New networks are created, old ones are broken. New frames of understanding are created, new stories are told and new explanations are offered. However, which stories get taken up and retold depends partly on their ability to explain but also partly on their ability to entertain.

Downing has argued that the flow of events and the unfolding of the story lines and plots can reinforce each other to create an emotional momentum. This momentum can be both positive (the feel good factor) or negative (the feel bad factor). Management teams, consultants and politicians will often try to interpret events to create a particular momentum. I will discuss in a moment how you can do this, but for now be aware you will hear about events and interpret messages in one plot line and that any message you send out to your team will be interpreted within these plot lines.

Logistics

There is one final layer that we have to examine. The simple mechanics of passing a message from one person to another. TJ Allen (quoted in Schein, 1988) has reported that proximity plays a crucial role in communication. He found that communication was directly related to physical distance amongst staff in a number of laboratories and that once the distance exceeded 40 metres communications dropped away to virtually zero. Naturally, in order to overcome this, formal meetings are set up which put people into proximity with each other so that communication can take place or messages are committed to paper or we have to pick up a phone. However, all of this means that the communication acquires a degree of formality and loses some of its spontaneity.

Allen's central point is well made: the further people are away from each other, the less likely the informal communication will be. In an enterprise as large, sprawling and complex as the NHS, it's small wonder that people are being overwhelmed with meetings and memos all striving to overcome the chasms created by the sheer magnitude of the operation. It is a lesson that has implications for any dispersed team. If your multi-disciplinary team is large, the problem of lack of proximity can be compounded by the number of people involved. Trying to broadcast the same message to a large number of people at the same time becomes much more difficult.

Making Your Communication Better

Trying to reconcile the different language sub-sets, the modes of language, the plot lines people will apply and the logistics of space and time may be causing your head to spin. If so give yourself a KISS and Keep It Simple Stupid. Use a simple message and repeat it because the chances are that somewhere in the swirl of language sub-sets, preferred communication modes, different plot lines and logistics it is going to mangled by someone.

Team members communicating with each other

Managers create contexts in which their staff can perform. Creating an environment in your team which cuts through the communications muddle is one of the most important contexts you can create. What you are seeking to do is to encourage your team to listen to each other and for you to listen to them.

Unfortunately in many multi-disciplinary teams the dominant communication model is a debate. In a debate a series of arguments are made. The problem is that often at the end of a debate what you have are a series of arguments. One of the main reasons that people don't listen is because they are already thinking about what they are going to say in reply. Communication is not a game of ping-pong where the object is to hit the ball back as hard as possible. It is about sharing understandings and expertise.

What you are seeking to foster is dialogue; that is, people listening to each other and understanding and respecting the basis on which the particular point is being made.

Much of this listening environment can be created by the tone you set as leader. Do you positively encourage participation from all members of the team or do you sit back and expect people to say things? Do you encourage a questioning and testing environment? Do you demonstrate that you listen to what people tell you? Take time out during your next team meeting and listen to the way your team are communicating with each other. Are they playing verbal ping-pong or paying attention to each other's point of view?

One of the key skills to develop in yourself and your team is that of summarizing. That is, the ability to play back to someone what you have heard them say. This requires you to pay attention to what they have said and show that you have understood it correctly. If you can summarize what someone has said, by definition you have listened to them.

Many teams are using group-ware on their PCs to improve their communication. Teams who have experimented with joint patient notes report that it improves their communication, although they have had to tread carefully around issues of patient confidentiality.

Finally, be open with your team about the complexities of bringing diverse disciplines together and the way that language can divide us. It is my experience that the more these process issues are made transparent, the more people understand the way their team works. And if I understand why something is difficult, I am more likely to put in the effort to do something about it.

You communicating with other people

When I am thinking about communicating something to someone I plan it out in three easy stages:

1. What am I trying to say?
2. Who am I trying to say it to?
3. How can I say it to them in ways that they will hear it?

Key messages

When planning what you are going to say, and it does need planning, focus on what your key messages are. In the deafening, relentless bombardment of exhortation, recrimination, requests and instructions that pounds away day after day in the NHS, what is the really important thing you want your target audience to take away? A key message is something that you want them to fully absorb and implement over a period of time. Telling your staff that the team meeting next week will start at 3 pm not 2.30 pm is not a key message. Telling them 'if something goes wrong, tell me straight away' is a key message because it is one that you will repeat over a matter of months.

Limit yourself to a maximum of five key messages per year. Any more than that and the impact will be dissipated. You might decide to have one about the way they work together, one about the teams goals, one about celebrating success, one about your management approach and one which is an organizational one. Do take the time to write them out and work on the form of words until you are happy you have got them right. Positive messages work better than negative ones, so avoid don'ts and emphasize dos. Short words and short sentences are always easier to understand than long words and long sentences. They are also much easier to remember. Use active verbs not passive ones. Be direct in the way you address them, so talk about 'we' and 'you' rather than 'the patient' and 'the organization'. Once you have got them right, start using them and keep on about them for at least 12 months. If your team aren't sick of hearing them yet, they haven't heard them enough! If you decide to add a new one, drop one of the existing ones.

Target audiences

A common mistake is to think that a key message is a 'one size fits all T-shirt'. It is not. A key message needs to be tweaked to the needs of the particular audience that is hearing it. For example, on finance, the key message from your boss might be don't bust the budget. With your team you might repackage this as we need to spend £x plus or minus 1 per cent. In other words we mustn't go over, but we don't want to undershoot either. For patients, the message might be your money is being well spent. This is not sophistry, trying to say one thing to one group and something else to another. It is a recognition, as I have tried to make clear, that different groups will hear different things, are interested in different things and need to be addressed in different ways.

When communicating with patients pay particular attention to using everyday English or, put another way, talk and write clearly.

Different media

There are a wide variety of methods you can use to transmit the messages you want to get across. You can use:

- word of mouth;
- written publications;
- cartoons;
- posters;
- postcards;
- reports;
- letters;
- memos.

And so forth. The look of the message sends important signals as well as the message itself. A poorly reproduced photocopy won't carry the same punch as something which is crisply printed. You might decide that the photocopy is OK for internal uses where it reinforces messages about not wasting money on fripperies, but you prefer to have cleanly printed material for the general public because it sends a positive message about the importance of quality and pride both to staff and to the public.

In choosing your words, bear in mind the impact of the language sub-sets, the value systems that lie behind them and the modes of language we all use. If you have a specific person or small group in mind, you can shape your message so that it fits their preferred style. But what about a situation where you don't know exactly who is going to be listening in? The rule of thumb is to assume that you will have all modes, all language sub-sets and all value systems in your audience and to use a variety of expressions so that at some point you are addressing everyone in their preferred style. In writing this book I have deliberately mixed the content of the case studies and the mode of language to take account of the variety of people who will be reading it.

Finally, as the saying goes, keep on message. Keep sending out the same clear messages over a period of time using a variety of media and they will get through.

Evaluating the Outcome

It is always worth taking time to see how effective your communication is. You can go for a full-blown communications audit and this can have its uses, but there are also things that you can do as you are going along which won't cost you anything. For example, listen to the conversations between staff. Are they using the key messages that you want to be transmitted? Take a snapshot survey in one of your team meetings: ask people how effective the present communication system is for them individually. Chat to patients and ask them what are the things they want to know about. As with all forms of evaluation, using several different thermometers even with quite small samples can give you very valuable insights into what is going on out there.

Conclusion

The most important attribute any manager can have is the ability to understand what their staff are communicating to them.

Only by hearing what staff are saying and watching what they are doing can you build up a three-dimensional sense of the world you are trying to manage. Once you have mapped this world and located your team within it, you can accurately target your communication with them by speaking to them in their language.

And finally, don't forget to repeat the message just in case it hasn't got through to someone!

Chapter 8

Cultures in Multi-disciplinary Teams

Introduction

A short while ago my mum had a spell of three admissions to hospital in the space of two months. Naturally I got to know the hospital quite well. It was an old building built at the end of the 19th century in the centre of the city. You enter up a flight of stone steps, walk through a lobby and then either turn left or right to walk down a short corridor to the wards. At either end of the ground-floor corridor were two Nightingale wards, each with 24 beds arranged in ranks of 12 against the wall with the nurses' station at the end. To protect the guilty, I shall call the ward on the right of the lobby Apple and the ward on the left of the lobby Peach. The first time she was admitted, my mum ended up in Apple. After a week or so she was discharged. She said she had never been so glad to get out of a hospital. The staff were rude, inattentive and gave the impression that the patients were a trial. A couple of weeks later, she was readmitted. This time to Peach. I was somewhat apprehensive about what I would find. The contrast could not have been greater. The staff were friendly, concerned, took time to chat to me and it was clear that they were not putting on a show. In the end my mum was quite sorry to leave. Two wards in the same building separated by 20 yards at most, with the same staff to patient ratios, the same organizational mission statement on the wall, the same physical conditions, working with the same consultants, with the same pay and reward structure and yet two completely different outcomes. Although there was no real difference in the quality of the medical care provided, there was a huge difference in the patient's experience.

What made the difference? The working culture that the manager of the wards had encouraged or allowed to develop. As a manager of a multi-disciplinary team you have a responsibility to ensure that the culture you encourage and tolerate reflects the values of involvement, support and care that make for good health care.

This chapter looks at the following points:

- what an organizational culture is;
- analysing the culture your team is operating within at the moment;
- the role of professional cultures in multi-disciplinary teams;
- how you can make cultures work for you.

What Is a Culture?

An organizational culture is a multi-layered system of collective beliefs. These beliefs may or may not be conscious but they help to shape, or for some writers determine, the way an organization conducts itself. In more everyday terms, it can be taken to mean the way we do things round here. This will include the way we relate to our colleagues, the myths and stories we weave about our organization and the relationships we have with patients. There are four main aspects to an organizational culture (see Figure 8.1). These are:

- norms – what's normal behaviour round here?
- beliefs – what staff think they are there to do and what staff think other people are there to do;
- values – the things that people think are important;
- metaphors – the symbols and signs we use to communicate with each other and the rest of the world.

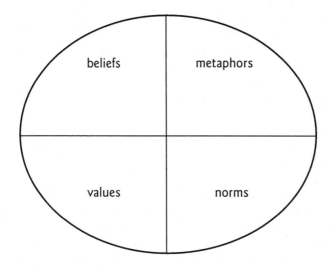

Figure 8.1 Aspects of organizational culture

The easiest way to explore these concepts and the way they relate to each other is to diagnose the culture you have at the moment.

The Culture Audit

Norms

Norms are the routine ways in which we live our lives and do our jobs. For example, do meetings start on time or do they regularly start ten minutes late? Is asking for advice a normal behaviour or are people expected to get on with it? What happens on people's birthdays? Does the celebrant buy everyone cakes? How are new staff initiated into the team? Is there some ceremony that people have to go through? And so on. Once you start looking for these small routines in your team you will be surprised by how many there are. Norms help to bind us together. They help us to anticipate what we can expect of other people and what they expect of us. We saw in the chapter on team building how important the creation of norms is to an effective team.

Norms can and are challenged by team members in the storming phase until a new norm takes over. For example, up until the 1970s smoking was generally permissible in meetings. By the mid-1980s this norm was being increasingly challenged and there would often be a vote on whether people wanted a smoke-free meeting. Now the norm has completely reversed. The expectation is that meetings will be smoke-free.

Beliefs

If norms are about surface behaviours, beliefs are the rational thinking patterns which underpin them. Beliefs are what we think we are there to do and what other people think we are supposed to do. For example, a doctor may believe that patients are only concerned with the quality of clinical care they receive and that therefore all doctors should devote themselves exclusively to study of the treatment of disease through drugs and surgery and not to be sidetracked into complementary approaches to medicine.

We organize our beliefs into coherent arguments so that there is some consistency. I might believe that all team members have an equal vote in team meetings and that if a decision is carried by a majority of one, then everyone must go along with it. You might believe that, in order to be effectively implemented and to maintain team unity, votes should be decided by a two-thirds majority. We both share many of the same values (of which more in a moment), but we have organized them into two different belief systems.

Beliefs can be altered. This is often by the presentation of empirical data. I believe that a procedure is both safe and effective because it has been thoroughly tested. I will continue to use it until you can change my mind by demonstrating that the testing was flawed or that there is another approach, equally well validated, which produces better results. Common beliefs are another of the structures that help to turn a group of individuals into a team. If we believe that we are an effective team because we can see an improvement in patient outcomes, then this will help to bind us together. Negative beliefs can also hold people together. A common enemy can be a useful team-building tool. If I can convince you that my enemy is your enemy then it will be much easier to convince you that we should work together to defeat that enemy.

Values

Beliefs are rooted in the rational, values are rooted in the emotional. They are our most deep-seated feelings about the world. Values are expressed through beliefs but they are not the same as beliefs. I may say 'I believe in fair play' but seeking to change my mind with rational argument won't necessarily work. With values we are in the realm of ethics and morality. I may take actions which are irrational because I believe they are the right thing to do.

Values and values systems are the most enduring part of any culture because they are the most difficult to change. I am passionately committed to my values and so are you. This means that they are often the source of the most fundamental conflicts within multi-disciplinary teams. Disentangling arguments about beliefs and values when your team is storming can be particularly difficult because, as we have noted above, people will express values as rational beliefs. As team manager you need to keep in touch with the emotions in the room: does it feel like people are banging heads together in a constructive way or is someone about to say 'well, you're just prejudiced'?

Symbols and metaphors

Symbols are the signs we use to communicate with each other and the rest of the world. A metaphor links two independent objects together directly. For example, this organization is a ship or my team is an elephant. We use symbols and metaphors extensively in our work to express what we think about ourselves, what the organization thinks about us and what I think about you. They are the mechanisms by which we transmit messages about our norms, values and beliefs. However, the messages they carry are open to interpretation and therefore the meanings they carry can be and are contested in organizations. For example, I may describe my team as an elephant because it is large and wise and in the jungle of our organization it reigns supreme. You may associate an elephant with being large and grey, taking nearly two years to give birth to a new idea and in grave danger of extinction from poachers.

Symbols and metaphors are important to you as a team manager. First, they give you a clue about the state of mind of the team members as individuals and as a group. Second, they give you a means to reinforce the messages you want to get across. You can contest the meanings just like anyone else.

Symbols and metaphors take three main forms. These are:

- Verbal, for example, jargon; the style and form of memos and letters; nicknames for people and equipment; legends and cautionary tales; jokes; beliefs and rumours; slogans and traditional sayings; ceremonial speeches.
- Activities, for example, play and games; practical jokes and initiations; celebrations and parties; gestures; food sharing; rituals and rites of passage; staff meetings, time outs and ceremonies; conventionalized techniques for doing jobs; customs.
- Objects, for example, the design of work space and furnishings; the quality and allocation of equipment; organization charts, manuals; bulletin boards (location and aesthetics); posters, photos and other memorabilia on display; standard dress and uniforms; decoration of one's workspace or equipment; graffiti.

A health authority in a big city had to make one-fifth of its staff redundant at the end of the financial year because of a funding crisis. As part of the cut they dispensed with their receptionists. Members of the public visiting this health authority, which is responsible for the health care of a quarter of a million people and the expenditure of £130 million of taxpayers' money every year, now walk into a deserted reception and are met by a sign above a telephone which asks them to ring an extension number for assistance.

The first time we go into an organization or team we will be acutely aware of these symbols. Because we know little or nothing about them we are drinking up as much data as we can find. Familiarity with people and environment means that we do not notice the way things look or are done. Next time you go into your workplace, take a moment to look and listen afresh because the next visitor will be a patient or a purchaser: what do the symbols and metaphors that you see and hear tell you about your organization and your team?

Professional Cultures

To make a multi-disciplinary team really effective, you need to make professionals coming from very different and sometimes conflicting professional cultures work together. A professional culture is the verbal expressions, activities and objects which help to identify someone as a doctor, nurse, or social worker. They are founded upon beliefs about what is important to a patient. They draw a boundary around 'us' which we can see and everyone else can see. Once you have been brought into the circle, a number of things happen.

First, you become part of the tradition of your profession and you can rightly take pride in the achievements of your colleagues down the years. Typically, entry into a profession is marked by a period of study (activity) where you acquire the main elements of your profession's body of knowledge. As I have noted before, the organization of intellectual disciplines and the professions which flow from them have allowed specialization and the development of detailed knowledge which have greatly contributed to the development of care. Once you have become a part of that profession you too can make your contribution to the sustenance and development of that body of knowledge. One of the things that people miss when they work in multi-disciplinary teams is the opportunity to meet their peers, to discuss cases from within their own world view and to have the chance to go that bit deeper into their subject.

Second, you also learn how to think like a member of your profession. For a doctor this might be about the centrality of treating the patient's disease. For a nurse, it might be the importance of caring for the whole person. The values and beliefs that you hold shape and constrain the way your knowledge can develop. This constraint is two-edged. The positive side is that it tells you what's important and therefore what you should focus on. The negative side is that it may cause you to underestimate evidence and opinion that does not conform to your core belief.

Some years ago I attended a conference on community care where a GP speaker commented on the lack of a common model for provision and argued that this demonstrated that we did not know how to 'do' community care. His point was, and is, a valid one and I thought his interpretation was interesting. Later I was discussing this contribution with a social worker who dismissed the argument literally with a wave of hand. 'It's the medical model of care. It's only by putting it in a social context that we'll make progress.' The issue is not who was right or wrong about whether the medical model of care has produced more benefit than the social model of care. The point being that no real dialogue could take place because the world views and the way they were shaping the minds of the protagonists were getting in the way.

> Protocols seemed to be developing a permission culture in the team. No one would do anything unless it was written down. People were getting a bit narrow-minded about their jobs. I was determined that we weren't going to let that attitude develop because it could only deflect us from our primary professional duty to provide the best for our patients.
>
> (Manager, Community Mental Health Team)

Finding the right balance between allowing people to remain a nurse or a doctor and the need to bring those skills into a generic whole is the very stuff of managing a multi-disciplinary team successfully. That is, creating an environment where staff can work together on what the specific contribution of each profession can be to the whole team.

Making Culture Work for You

First, a caveat. As I have tried to make clear, culture is a dynamic and multi-layered phenomenon which does not lie at the beck and call of any individual or group of individuals. You cannot change the culture like a pair of socks. Nevertheless, there are things that you can do which will help you get closer to where you want your team to be.

Successful cultural transformations are nearly always about co-opting and adapting existing symbols and metaphors and playing them back to people in new combinations and with new messages. In short, you talk to people in their own language. One of the most successful examples of this was the way the early Christian Church adopted pagan gods, feasts and festivals and reinvented them into the Christian canon.

There is a common tendency among most multi-disciplinary teams to let the decision-making drift back to the doctors. Observe how decisions get taken in your team. Whose opinion really counts? Who is contributing to the discussion? Is anyone missing? Is there a positive commitment to the decision or silent acquiescence? Who is sitting at the head of the table?

If you want genuine multi-disciplinary decision-making, then you have to keep on working at it. It won't happen by itself. The trick is to keep on the lookout for objects, verbal expressions and architecture that are in tune with the overall culture you are try-ing to develop. You could for example rotate the role of chair in your meetings around the team or encourage a first name cul-ture rather than addressing people as Dr Smith and Nurse Jones.

This includes jumping on things which do not fit the culture you want. Be particularly aware of the 'I blame whoever is not in the room' syndrome. A common enemy can be a force for unity within a team. However, part of your job is to ensure that if there are enemies they are not people with whom the team has to work. It can be a cop-out for teams to blame their own mis-fortune on the actions of others. It is positively dangerous when they start blaming people they work with from another depart-ment or organization. If there is a genuine grievance, then you need to ensure action is taken to sort it out. If it is just whinging, then you need to control it and set an alternative example of what the approach ought to be. This does not need to be a major song and dance, small actions repeated again and again will get the message over. Think of it as routine maintenance: repainting the front of your house so that the windows aren't exposed to the weather and start to rot.

Overall, then, the main strategy is one of evolution and grad-ual change rather than a big bang approach. Lots of small steps are easier to achieve and if they are heading in the same basic direction will achieve progress. However, there are two oppor-tunities where rapid progress can be made and both should be seized.

The first is when you are creating a new team. There is an opportunity from the start to set the tone you want to establish within the team. You may want to emphasize themes of participation, patient-centred services and mutual respect between colleagues. The best way to do this is not to stand at the front of your team with a loud hailer demanding that they show respect for their colleagues. Much better to let the team set rules (you are trying to encourage participation) and then your role becomes the keeper of the rule book that they have written. With the never-ending sweep of restructuring and reorganization, there are usually plenty of opportunities to start afresh. Most restructurings are driven by the need to cope with shortages of money. There is no reason why they cannot be used to try to alter behaviours and attitudes of staff so that they and their patients have a better time. This may seem naïve when people are frightened for their jobs and sick of being messed about, but if you don't try, they will still be frightened for their jobs and sick of being messed about. Being honest and upfront with people, you get the best out of them.

The second opportunity is when a new member joins your team. New starters acquire knowledge about the organization/team from two sources: formal training (induction, etc) and informal socialization (the chat about how things work around here, who to avoid, who is good, etc). Mixed messages will stand out like a sore thumb. If I hear rhetoric about participation and involvement in the formal induction, but the gossip around the coffee machine says that the boss takes all the decisions, then immediately as a new starter I get a sense of a culture that says one thing but does another.

Conclusion

The culture in your team will be one of the most critical influences on how the members of your team work with patients and each other. It is an area that you need to actively manage.

In the total quality school of management there is a Japanese word, *kaizen*, which is usually translated as meaning continuous improvement. In fact, a better translation is improving everything, everywhere, all of the time. Good enough managers describe it as chipping away at it.

Chapter 9

I Wouldn't Start
from Here

Introduction

It would be nice to think that most teams work well most of the time. In many cases they do, but there are always some which are not performing to their potential. A dysfunctional team is not necessarily a team in crisis. It can be simply a team which is muddling along and not fulfilling its potential. Under-performance can be like a cancer. It slowly eats away at people's confidence and motivation until one day you have a team in full-blown crisis.

Whether multi-disciplinary teams are more prone to dysfunction than uni-disciplinary teams is a moot point. Uni-disciplinary teams may be more efficient on the surface, but effective modern health care needs the range of talents that multi-disciplinary teams can provide. Certainly there are many more things to go wrong with a multi-disciplinary teams than for a uni-disciplinary team. The additional tensions that different structures and cultures can provide result in people working together less effectively, particularly in a demanding environment like the NHS.

This chapter looks at situations which you wish you had not inherited but you've got landed with, and what you can do about them. Using the model of multi-disciplinary teams set out in Chapter 1, we will look in particular at three roots of dysfunctional multi-disciplinary teams.

- structures;
- cultures;
- people.

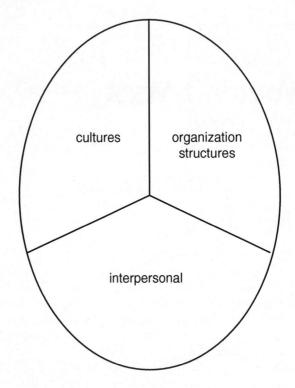

Figure 9.1 Effectiveness in a multi-disciplinary team

Why Are Poorly Performing Teams a Bad Thing?

When you are faced with having to sort out a mess, particularly when it is someone else's mess, there is always a small voice whispering in your ear: it's not worth it, it's too difficult, keep your head down and look for a new job. It is worth spending a short time reviewing the impact dysfunctional teams have on their members and their patients.

Patients and their carers are often acute observers of staff. It is pretty easy to tell when people are not happy with each other and their situation. Even if the arguments are held behind closed doors, a frosty atmosphere and sharp words will be picked up by patients. Moreover, disorganization and lack of communication leading to patients being ignored for long periods or several practitioners arriving at the patient's home at the same time are not impressive. This will quickly create a perception of poorer levels of care. A team which is not looking after itself is not in a good position to look after others. If you don't listen to your colleagues, why should you listen to the patient? Furthermore, a dysfunctional team will give the patient mixed messages about their care. This can cause unnecessary confusion and anxiety for the patient and their family.

Dysfunctional teams also make people less happy, more stressed and less effective in their work. No one actively wants to work in an unhappy work environment. We want to enjoy the work we do. Sadly this is a situation fewer of us are now experiencing at work. There has been a 500 per cent increase in time off for stress-related sickness since 1950 and 44 per cent of the workforce report coming home exhausted. For both men and women, doctors and nurses appear in the top ten occupational groups most likely to commit suicide. Work is always harder when you are not enjoying it.

So, as a manager, you have a responsibility to tackle a dysfunctional team because it will improve the experience and health of both your patients and your staff. Now that is a target that is worth shooting at.

Why Do Teams Become Dysfunctional?

Teams usually become dysfunctional because of a mixture of internal neglect and external change. If people do not look after the internal relationships, do not listen to each other, do not respect each other, disillusion and cynicism will follow. A dysfunctional team risks not sharing information and risks making decisions on patient care without all the relevant information. And even well-functioning teams can be blown away by major

And even well-functioning teams can be blown away by major external change. There's nothing like a restructuring to throw everything out of kilter.

Like some personal relationships that have gone bad, it can be difficult sometimes for a team and the people in it to break out of the dysfunctional pattern they are in. In some way the dysfunction fits the current pattern of interests and relationships in a team or an organization. People in organizations are very quick learners. We learn how to avoid blame, to survive, how to operate within a particular organizational system, to politic, how much risk to take, when to be deferential. If we feel that to challenge the present position will place us at risk, it will be much easier to muddle along complaining as we go, than to take decisive action. This is particularly the case for junior members of the team whose position is always most at risk and who have the least power to positively improve things, but a lot of negative power in terms of blocking, going slow and not being helpful.

These behaviours are not just logical actions, they are driven by emotions: blame is painful, we need allies and friends, we don't want to be singled out. Fear and anxiety contribute to how people interpret meaning. It is easy to see people falling into the tragedy story line I discussed in Chapter 7, where I am the victim of other people's actions and therefore people will feel sorry for me. Whereas, if I take some action, I may generate conflict, opposition and criticism.

Organizational and Structural Causes

The NHS is like a rope being pulled in two directions. At one end of the rope are the expectations and ambitions of high-quality services provided close to home where almost anything is possible. The mantra of 'the best health service in the world' is a source of inspiration and pride and a huge weight around the neck of the service. Patient expectations have risen steadily over the last few years. This has been driven by advances in medicine, the rise in the consumer society and the growing expectation that we can have whatever we want and we can have it now. We no longer expect to be told that we cannot have a choice or that there is a queue. On the other end of the rope is the constant pull of diminishing tax revenues available to pay for these growing elections that we won't pay the tax levels required for high-quality public services. We want more for less. And so the rope gets stretched by these contradictory forces and it is the task of managers in the NHS to perform the balancing act and to find the middle way even when one doesn't really exist.

The consequence of the contradiction of rising demand for services and static or falling resources is that people seeking to protect their own services against an external threat will get embroiled in turf wars. These disputes can be between organizations, department and professions. They inhibit the freedom to manoeuvre a multi-disciplinary team and contribute to an atmosphere of siege where the first priority is to defend the status quo and the current hierarchies.

Tackling the organizational and structural causes of dysfunction from a relatively lowly position is hard. As a manager you may be placed in an uncomfortable position. On the one hand, being asked to implement organizational agendas which you or your team are hostile towards; on the other, trying to get your team to fulfil its potential. These are dilemmas which can challenge your own deeply held views about the way health care ought to be provided. You end up feeling like you are the rope being pulled in two directions. Welcome to management.

The only advice I can offer is to remain resourceful. Using a technique called the third position may be helpful. This is where you analyse a situation through your own eyes (the first position), then look at it through the eyes of your team (the second position). Finally, you analyse it from the position of a benign, helpful observer looking in from the outside (the third position). What tips, advice and encouragement would this observer give you? You are still a free agent responsible for your own actions with the ability to make things happen. You need to carve out a space which is recognizably yours and which you feel comfortable with by working hard on getting your team to perform well and to deliver the organizational objectives you have been given. If you can deliver on these, then you have the opportunity to add some value in the way you do your work.

The Chinese pictogram for crisis brings together the symbols for danger and opportunity. Successful managers stay resourceful. Organizational and structural conflict does offer some opportunities. The endless round of restructuring does mean that the old way of doing things can be challenged. Most good managers have a couple of pet projects tucked away in the bottom drawer of their desk. They are the sorts of thing that can be quickly worked up into a business case to try out new ways of working, or new forms of relationships. You might think of this as strategic opportunism. You are pursuing a long-term agenda about what the shape of your organization should be and you grab any opportunity that comes along to try to put it into practice.

A hill-walking friend of mine described the awful realization that he was lost on a moor in deteriorating weather. For a few moments he was terror-struck. 'I had a choice. I could either say I'm lost, give up and wait for someone to find me. Perhaps they would, perhaps they wouldn't. Or I could say I don't know where I am but I have a map, a compass and my eyes, so all I have to do is to marry up the information on my map with the information from my eyes.' It took him half an hour, but he worked out where he was and got safely home. His postscript to the story is also interesting. 'Trying to work out where I was made me feel better because at least I was doing something.'

Dysfunctions Resulting from Cultures

The previous chapter discussed the types of conflict and tensions that arise from the domination of uni-disciplinary training and education and the mind-sets which emerge from them.

In tackling culturally rooted dysfunctions you will need to make a positive case for multi-disciplinary working. It is a more exciting, challenging way of working and one which offers better care to patients and more fun to staff. It is also more demanding, but then making the future has never been easy.

Dysfunctions arising from culture will make big demands on you as a manager. You have to model the culture you want to encourage: a case of doing as I do and not just as I say. As we saw in the last chapter, professional and organizational cultures reach deep into the souls of practitioners. You and your team need to find the balance between respecting the achievements of the uni-disciplinary approach and the further opportunities that multi-disciplinary working offers.

Dysfunctions rooted in culture will often manifest themselves in communication. This is partly mis-communications arising from Pietroni's language sub-sets and partly the dialogue of the deaf that argues I won't listen to them because they are not the same tribe as me.

Poor communication

If you have a team that is dysfunctional, getting them into the same room at the same time to storm it out is nearly always a good first step, and if not the first step, then certainly the second. But do remember that while you are aware that the storming behaviour is perfectly normal and healthy, there may be members of the team who see it as an unmitigated disaster. So share your knowledge about cultures and team development. The more the whole team are aware of the processes which are influencing them working together, the quicker they can develop the maturity you are seeking.

Dysfunctions Arising from People

There is always a tendency to blame people. It may be that organizational, structural or cultural issues are being attributed to people being difficult, and you need to be aware of this possibility. Nevertheless interpersonal problems do arise.

There are four main areas where people can make things tricky for the team:

- Staff turnover and instability.
- Getting stuck as a team.
- Numbers.
- Personalities.

Turnover and instability

Turnover and instability of team membership are an endemic problem in many parts of secondary care in the NHS. The arrival problem in many parts of secondary care in the NHS. The arrival of new team members always shifts the balance within the team. They bring a different mix of skills, knowledge and personality to the team. Each time the existing roles and relationships have to be subtly renegotiated between you and the new member, also between existing team members. The centre of gravity of the team shifts each time there is a change of personnel. As manager of the team you will need to ensure that the transition from new boy or girl to old hand is as smooth as possible. Entry into the team is one of the most important phases in any team member's life. I have discussed in Chapter 8 on culture the way this happens, both formally and informally. You might think about the rituals or rites of passage that new staff members will have to go through before they 'officially' come on board. The induction programme you put people through will be an important part of this but why not stretch the concept beyond doing a tour of the fire exits and being shown how to operate the coffee machine and add something which is important and of value to integrating into the team?

> We had a new district nurse joining our practice. And we were desperate for her. The post had been vacant for nearly nine months. We had to strive hard to avoid the temptation to just chuck her straight in to relieve the pressure on the rest of us. We made sure that in her first month she spent time, good time not just five minutes, with each of the GPs, the other community nurses, social services, and so on. Although she was a bit frustrated by it to start with, she's a very practical person who gets on with things, she told me later that the time she spent getting to know her colleagues in those first few weeks has been invaluable.
>
> (General Practitioner)

There is no hiding the fact that managing a team which is permanently in transition is difficult. It can be hugely frustrating for existing team members to keep going back over the forming stage again and again. And you don't want to have to renegotiate the team's norms every time someone new comes in. There have to be some points of stability. The culture that you have created can be one of those points of stability. You will need to lis-

Which story line (see Chapter 7) are they using? Reminding members both old and new of the progress they have made can be another. Clear goals and targets will help to settle people in and make them feel like they are contributing quickly. Be clear about the things you think will be important to get new people on board and keep the old hands up to speed. In the end it's the same point I have made several times already: a succession of small actions over a period of time which all hang together is more effective in building a team than a one-off big bang.

Static teams

Ironically enough, static teams can be just as much of a problem as teams with constant turnover. In some ways they are more difficult because the collective memory of 'how we've done things in the past' is that much shorter in a turnover team. It isn't possible to write an equals sign between static teams and stuck teams. Some of the best teams are those with strong and stable memberships. But where you have stable memberships, group think which I discussed in Chapter 6 becomes more of a problem and the team can become too comfortable and too dismissive of new ideas or ways of working.

In multi-disciplinary health care teams this can often translate itself into a drift back to the doctor making the decisions and everyone else implementing them. Powerful currents of history, education and expectation area always pushing against a fully multi-disciplinary approach. It takes an effort of will to keep the ship on course. Regular exposure to different ways of thinking and working is the best way to achieve this. This means the team as a whole doing new things together.

Rattling the bars of the cage does not need to be a confrontational or noisy process. You can just try some of these tactics:

- run a meeting in a different way;
- get a video or speaker in;
- visit other sites *en masse* or in series;
- start a new project;
- celebrate the end of an old one.

But if you don't have the challenge of new people coming in, you need to find ways of keeping things fresh and dynamic. Build it into your plan.

Size

In Chapter 2 I have already discussed the difficulties that size presents to many multi-disciplinary teams. Participation and communication become much more difficult when you are trying to do it with large numbers of people. The larger the group or meeting, the fewer the number of people who can take part in the discussion. Moreover, people tend to adopt more formal positions and attitudes in larger groups and meetings. Informality and exchange thrive on intimacy. If you are stuck with a large meeting, think about ways of breaking it up perhaps using some of the techniques discussed in Chapter 6.

There is no question that a team has to meet together on a regular basis to become and remain a team. This is over and above any operational communications meetings that are held. This should happen at least once a year and preferably twice a year. These get-togethers are to do team-related business about what you are doing and how you are doing it. Just on a very simple level people need to see who else is in their team.

Finding the time can be very difficult and finding a time to suit everyone can be nigh on impossible. The bigger the team, the more difficult it becomes. It then becomes a question of how important this team is. If it is important to them in the conduct of their work, they and you will find the time. If it isn't that important, then don't call this collection of individuals a team. There is nothing wrong with that. It is OK not to be in a team for everything.

Difficult people

What they do
Managers really earn their corn when they successfully manage 'difficult' people. This difficulty can be caused by a number of different factors or by a combination of them. Handling it, particularly when you can feel your own temper rising, makes real

demands on you. This is the sort of occasion when listening to the calming inner voice speaking from the third position offering tips and advice can be particularly helpful.

As with handling other situations the first step is diagnosis: what is the cause of the problem? Approaches vary from softly softly to the direct. Personally I veer increasingly to the direct. Direct doesn't have to be the same as blunt. The tone in which the inquiry is made will make a lot of difference but at least with a direct question like: 'you seem to be having some problem with the task, is that right?', everyone knows where they are. The direct approach will help you sort out the people who don't understand what you are asking them to do from the ones who understand perfectly well, but don't want to do it.

The second important check is whether the view or attitude being expressed is an individual one or one shared by a number or all of the team. If the difficult person is isolated within the team you may find the team helping you to manage the difficulty. On the other hand, if they are expressing the mainstream view within the team your strategy for managing it will be different.

What you are seeing may reflect a number of issues. Difficult people can create problems because of the following.

- They come with hidden agendas or different agendas.
- They lack trust, honesty or confidence.
- They lack a shared vision or common objectives or common values with the rest of the team.
- They are irrational or go on and on about the same thing – the broken record.
- They are sarcastic and make a joke of everything.
- They are angry, hostile or rude.
- They behave as if they are more important than the rest of the team or seek to dominate the group.
- They play games in the team.
- They actively resist your authority in the team either publicly or 'outside the room'.
- They have difficulty in handling a dual role – for example, being a professional and a manager.
- They attribute blame to others all the time.
- They try to avoid the issue - for example, by not defining the problem.
- They focus on the past and not the future.
- They are right.

These are types of behaviour but to deal with them effectively you need to tackle the underlying causes, not the presenting symptoms. In Chapter 2 I identified five factors that make teams successful. These were as follows.

- Clear goals.
- Clear roles.
- The right mix.
- Good working relationships.
- Something in it for the individual.

In diagnosing the cause of the difficult behaviour you are seeing, using this framework can help you understand better what is happening. For example, ask yourself the following questions:

- Is the problem a lack of clarity about the team's goals? Or are the goals perfectly clear, it's just that there is a fundamental dispute about whether they are the right goals?
- Do people understand what their role is? Is this the role in the team they want or aspire to? Are professional toes being trodden on?
- Does the individual have the confidence that they have the skills and knowledge to carry out their allotted tasks? One survey of stress found that the second highest cause, accounting for 19 per cent of cases, was lack of confidence.
- Is there a good working relationship between team members? Are you consistent and fair in your treatment of people or are you perceived to have favourites? Are the workloads and responsibilities fairly spread?
- Is the individual bored by the job they've got? Jaundiced because they didn't get a promotion? Just burnt out and in need of a rest?

Handling difficult behaviour

As you can see, this thing 'difficult behaviour' encompasses a vast array of causes. So what can you do to handle this type of behaviour? I cannot be prescriptive about what you should do. You will need to go with what you feel is right for the person you are dealing with, the circumstances you are working in and your particular style. However, I can underline one message: don't guess, ask.

Listening to your team both as a group and as individuals is something that people like me go on about endlessly. And people like you nod wisely and then make a decision and take action because that's what managers do. I know because I have done it myself. You want to be dynamic, in charge and not be exposed to some of the uncomfortable messages that may come back. I now have a little rule of thumb: when I think I know the answer, I get one more piece of data in just to make sure.

Having said that, one of the most difficult people to work with is the one who would always rather talk than do anything, as my colleagues occasionally remind me. There is a need to resolve the situation. A problem individual compromises the team's ability to provide high-quality health care. The patient and their family won't be interested in hard luck stories and personal tragedies. There are a number of different strategies you can choose from. You can try one of these tactics.

- Ignore it – if you have a game player deliberately looking to pick an argument, then not responding, gives them nothing for them to play with.
- Confront directly – either quietly 'are you sure you are right?' or if a decision or action is urgent then more assertively, 'you are wrong and here are the reasons why.'
- Divert it or 'park' it into a conversation at a later stage where it can be dealt with – useful when you are pressed for time and the problem is important but not urgent. To be credible you must follow through on this.
- Try to understand it and describe it – problem behaviour is often caused by anxiety about something that can't quite be named. Talking it out is time-consuming but demonstrates commitment to the individual and their concern. It also absorbs the energy that was driving the problem.
- Consider the individual's future – occasionally it is necessary to move people on against their will. You may need to use the disciplinary mechanisms. Before you get to that stage, having a frank conversation with the individual might do the trick. Acknowledging the current situation is not productive for them, for you or for the patients and that there may be another working situation where they might feel happier can break open the situation. Do not act precipitately and do take advice from your personnel and HR specialists. The rest of the

team will be watching closely because they might be next. The way you move people out of your team is an important marker of how important you think people are in your team.

Dysfunctional Leaders

Last but by no means least, we come to the dysfunctional leader. All of the things which can be true of a team can be true of their manager. You too can be demotivated and disoriented by the constant bombardment of change. You can be stuck and lacking any fresh ideas or energy. You can displace onto others at work problems at home. Given the workload you've got, it's hardly surprising. The research evidence is that 25 per cent of managers take work home seven days per week. The average lunch 'hour' now lasts 30 minutes and is falling. You can't manage other people properly if you can't manage yourself. So make time for yourself. Book in those holidays and take them. If you've got too much work to do in a reasonable number of hours, then weed your in-tray. Ask the following questions.

- What is absolutely essential to you and your team being able to do their job? Who could do this? One of the implicit values in team work is sharing the load fairly, so share it. Giving people new responsibilities and opportunities is the way they can develop their career.
- What has to be done to keep the organization off your back?
- What offers some extra value to you or to members of your team?

Then throw the rest of it away.

Conclusion

As we have seen, most dysfunctional teams are not entirely populated by malcontents and baddies. They are often desperate for someone to provide some leadership and support. As manager, you have to help them make sense of what is happening around them. Revisiting the team's goals and its norms and values is them. Revisiting the team's goals and its norms and values is never a bad place to start. Naturally, a dysfunctional team won't be able to make the time to have this discussion, that's why it's dysfunctional. Your job is to make it happen. Believe me, a bit of determination and drive sustained over a period will make a difference.

Managing a difficult team, individual or situation or all three at the same time is hard work. Use your friends and colleagues for support. Don't bottle up the stress, let it out. I have a friend who swears by arcade games. He reckons 15 minutes on a really gory shoot 'em up is worth any number of hours of counselling. You might prefer talking to someone. Everyone is different and so are you.

There is a neat distinction drawn by some writers between puzzles and problems which may help. A puzzle is something to which there is a technical solution if you just look hard enough. A problem is a problem precisely because it is not solvable.

Good enough managers understand there are three boxes that issues at work can be put into:

- those you control;
- those you can influence;
- those you can nothing do about.

They put their energy into sorting through the first two boxes and leave the third one to arguments down the pub.

Chapter 10

Developing Yourself and Your Team

Introduction

The world of the NHS is undergoing continuous change. The needs of patients change as new conditions and diseases spread through the population. New drugs and clinical techniques are becoming available as our knowledge and technologies develop. As we have noted before, these changes are one of the primary driving forces propelling the multi-disciplinary approach forward. As individuals, we all need to stay on top of new developments and to adapt our practice to provide quality services to patients and to keep the job fresh for ourselves. The essence of multi-disciplinary working is learning from others. Reflection is a powerful weapon in your armoury to develop both individual and team practice.

This commitment to learning is built on a questioning attitude to practice: how can we do better? How can we improve? This type of open attitude is particularly valuable in multi-disciplinary settings because it enables practitioners to share their knowledge in an atmosphere of respect. It also lessens the risks of the type of miscommunication and misunderstanding that the interplay of Pietroni's language sub-sets can cause. And if we wish to involve patients and their families fully, we need to be able to draw out their stories and experiences. If we ask good questions of ourselves, we can ask good questions of the patients. A reflective practitioner quickly becomes a more effective practitioner.

Continuing education and development, then, are a prerequisite for effective and safe practice. This chapter looks at:

- how individuals learn;
- how teams learn;
- methods individuals and teams can use to make it happen.

How Individuals Learn

The learning ladder and the learning cycle

In discussing how adults learn I am going to use two models. The first is the learning ladder. This describes the four stages our knowledge travels through. These stages are as follows:

1. Unconscious incompetence.
2. Conscious incompetence.
3. Conscious competence.
4. Unconscious competence.

In other words, at first we don't even know that we lack a skill. As a young child, for example, a car is just driven for us. We do not know that there is a skill to doing it. Later, as a young teenager, we become aware that we lack the skill and knowledge to drive. When we become learner drivers acquiring the skills and knowledge we lack, we have to concentrate hard on every aspect of driving the car. Finally, as an experienced driver we internalize many of the skills to the extent we can suddenly 'wake up' and find that we have driven to work on auto-pilot.

The second model is that of the learning cycle. There are many variations on this. The one I use has three stages (see Figure 10.1). First, we accumulate experiences that we wish to understand: the review stage. This stage is important because in order to learn we have to be aware of the need to learn. Bad drivers cannot improve because they are not aware of needing to improve their performance. They may have become unconsciously competent in the skills needed to make the car move forward at a given speed. But they are unaware of the need to improve their road craft. In other words, they are unconsciously incompetent in relation to their road craft.

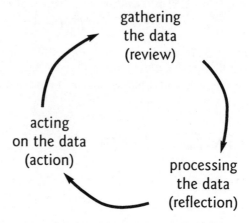

gathering
the data
(review)

acting
on the data
(action)

processing
the data
(reflection)

Figure 10.1 The learning cycle

Second, we place those experiences into some sort of framework: the reflection stage. Frameworks, models and theories all provide structures in which we can place and evaluate our evidence. These frameworks of understanding are based on our own previous experience, the things that we have been taught and ideas we have developed for ourselves.

Even if you do not explicitly apply a model as a way of understanding the data, you will still be using it implicitly. What you are doing when you are processing data is searching for the pattern which can be used to explain the phenomena. Models and frameworks are just a systematic way of doing that.

On the basis of the framework or model you are using, you will come to an understanding of the situation at hand. You will be able to develop predictions, or hypotheses, about what should happen next. Such predictions guide into the third phase of the learning cycle which is applying our knowledge and understanding in action: the action stage. The cycle of learning is now complete because these actions will create a new set of experiences that we strive to understand and make sense of.

The point about learning is that all three phases of the learning cycle need to be worked through for learning to take place. We must be aware of our experiences so that we can learn. We must place those experiences into some sort of framework or model to understand them. We must apply our knowledge in action in order to confirm our learning.

At various times in our lives we will focus on different phases in the cycle. The biggest learning curve in management is the week between the first Monday of your first management job and the second Monday. The torrent of experience can be quite overwhelming. But having survived the first week, it is possible to see patterns repeating themselves immediately in the second. When the stock of experiences has grown, it can be helpful to focus on acquiring structures and frameworks. The frameworks I have provided in this book will provide you with a start. You might get others from training or education programmes or through discussion with colleagues, friends and your team. Later you may want to focus on the action stage by carrying out some action research where you control the environment and what you do in order to test a particular hypothesis.

Wherever you focus and wherever you start, the point about the learning cycle is that it has to be completed if you are going to move up the learning ladder.

The reflective practitioner

The reflective practitioner is someone who actively works their way through the learning cycle in the course of their work. They seek to apply learning and insights of other people in their work and to develop their own insights and to share these with their colleagues. Reflective practice is the basic building block of scientific inquiry.

For example, suppose you want to check your management approach to your team against the team's needs. A reflective practitioner will first analyse the stage they have reached. The life cycle of teams we discussed in Chapter 3 will provide an analytical framework for your review and provide you with an understanding of where the team has reached. If, say, this is the norming stage, then the framework will offer some advice on the best role you can play and what you may expect to see next, in this case the team will display some storming behaviour. In other words, the model you are using is giving you information both on what action you might take now and what you can expect to happen next. Armed with this understanding, you will adopt the approach suitable for a team that is norming. But you won't stop there. You will remain open to the team's needs changing and be aware that your role will have to shift once the team begins storming.

The reality of the workplace

In the busy world of the NHS, time for preparation and planning is always under pressure. Many decisions get taken on the hoof. Mistakes and bruised egos can often result. Good enough managers are not frightened of making mistakes, but they hate making the same mistake twice. They know that the trick is to learn from these situations and to strive to avoid repeating them in the future.

The precise convergence of circumstances that you have just worked through won't recur again. However, something similar will. If your approach worked last time, use it again. If it didn't, try something different. Good enough management is about giving yourself the space to reflect on what you've done and to build on that experience. It is the reflection that moves you beyond trial and error.

You probably won't have any more time the next time you need to make a decision about action, but because you do your homework you are learning to make smarter decisions. Developing 'nous' like this is what turns a good enough manager into a getting better manager.

How Teams Learn

So much for how individuals learn. Do teams learn in the same way? The overall process of gathering experiences or data, processing that data using models and frameworks, and then acting on the conclusions reached holds good. However, the dynamics of the team mean that there are some significant differences.

When teams learn together they use four distinct techniques for learning. These are shown in Figure 10.2.

- Framing and reframing their understanding.
- Joint experimentation.
- Crossing boundaries.
- Integrating perspectives.

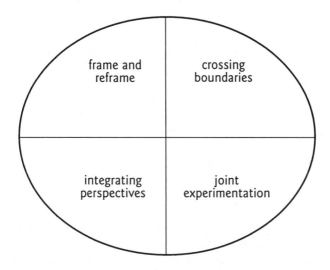

Figure 10.2 The ways teams learn

Teams will often use these techniques in sequence. They will often start by trying to frame a collective understanding of what they are seeing in front of them. This initial frame often fails to fully explain what is going on. The team will then reframe or reshape that understanding.

This process of framing and re-framing may well take some time to develop as the effects of Peitroni's language sub-sets and the effects of the uni-disciplinary professional cultures need to be worked through. In particular, teams which have not fully matured can find reframing particularly difficult. Several models may fit the data. The one that you and your team go with may be the one that best explains the phenomena or it could be the one that most closely fits your values. Models and frameworks are not neutral. They tell you what is important and help you to discriminate between the meaning in the data and mere noise. Different professions value different models and hence different parts of the data. Although a psychiatrist and a psychologist may have a great deal in common, they will still construct their understandings of the world in different ways.

The opportunity for the team to reframe their understanding gives you the leeway to make a quick start with a broad understanding without giving up the chance to develop that understanding later.

When moving into experimentation or action mode, the team will differ from the individual. In Chapter 6 we have already discussed the impact of satisficing, group think and risky think and the ways that these can shape the actions a team takes. More positively, multi-disciplinary teams can jointly develop hypotheses which they can test together. In health care, these hypotheses can be very rich, informed by a number of different perspectives. The human mind, body and spirit is a wonderfully complex and beautiful thing. Working and learning together in a multi-disciplinary team provides opportunities to stretch and integrate knowledge and understanding.

For teams which are struggling to gel, experimenting, testing or piloting approaches can be a valuable way of building trust, confidence and shared experience. As the team develops, individuals will feel increasingly confident about crossing boundaries and reaching out beyond their professions to trade ideas, information and views between each other. Some teams will find this relatively easy, others more bound up with the uni-professional model will reject the views of outsiders. Generally speaking, the more mature and effective a team becomes, the more willing it is to cross these mental, cultural, physical or organizational boundaries. When boundary crossing, team members will still be mainly operating individually or in small groups. As team manager this type of boundary crossing is the sort of behaviour and attitude that you want to encourage.

Integrating perspectives takes boundary crossing to the next level where the team as a whole synthesize their divergent views without resorting to compromise or some sort of voting system. Integrating perspectives does not rule out differences of opinion but there is a jointly developed and agreed solution. However many views there were during the process, by the end the team is of one mind.

Generally speaking, the more effective and mature the team, the more consistently they are using all four learning techniques of framing, experimenting, crossing boundaries and integrating perspectives. For individuals this can be a challenging and difficult process. In teams these are not processes which will arise automatically. As a manager it is part of your responsibilities to ensure that the team is learning about itself and its work. Encouraging your team members individually and collectively to use these approaches will help get them on the right track to maturity and effectiveness.

As your team develops, you will see the way they approach their learning change. In some ways this mirrors the forming, norming, storming, performing, mourning cycle we have already discussed. The three stages are shown in Figure 10.3. These are:

1. individualized learning;
2. shared learning;
3. joint learning.

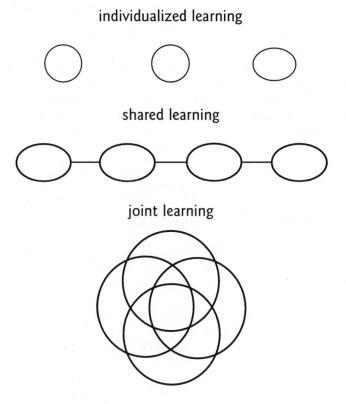

Figure 10.3 Stages in joint learning

At the individualized stage, team members are still working and learning in isolation from one another. Most of the learning is about data gathering and framing. There may be some experimenting but it will be done in ones and twos. There will not be much information sharing amongst the group.

Shared learning occurs when opportunities to learn together are taken up. This leads to team members developing shared understandings based on a common data pool. Frameworks of understanding will be developed together and there will be some boundary crossing to gather information and views. Joint experimentation will take place and information and views will flow across the team.

Joint learning occurs when the team as a whole negotiates shared meanings, values and beliefs which lead to an integration of perspectives. Boundaries are being crossed regularly and consistently. There is collective framing and reframing of issues and situations.

Most teams need encouragement and leadership from their managers to use all of these techniques. As they develop and mature and make more use of these techniques, so they will develop integrated understandings based on their rich mix of perspectives. Integrated, mature teams provide high-quality health care and a more enjoyable and stimulating work environment for their members.

Techniques for Learning

There are dozens of different techniques which you can use with individuals and with teams. I will discuss just seven. If you want more help with any of these techniques or to look at other ways of meeting development needs, talk to your local personnel and HR specialists. The seven techniques I will discuss are:

- Action learning.
- Clinical audit.
- PUNS and STUNS.
- Shadowing.
- Peer review.
- 360-degree feedback.
- Field-books.

Action learning

Action learning was originally developed by Reg Revans. It is a technique that involves groups of practitioners working together on real problems and issues. Revans has argued that learning is made up of a combination of 1) programmed knowledge – that which is in books, on web sites and is already known; and 2) questioning knowledge – that which we discover through asking questions.

Action learning focuses particularly on the development of questioning knowledge through discussion with our peers and colleagues. Action learning often takes place in small groups, sometimes called action learning sets, who meet at regular intervals over a period of time. The group will work on real problems and issues brought by group members. Individuals retain responsibility for sorting out their own issues or problems. The group as a whole will work to help the individual develop their understanding of the issue. The group's focus is on finding actions which the individual can take to tackle their issue.

Action learning is a powerful technique which is very closely allied to action research. It is based on the sort of discussions which practitioners will have anyway with their peers about specific problems and issues. It makes sure these discussions happen in a structured and supported way. The focus on action helps to make the learning practical rather than theoretical.

Clinical audit

There are many variations of clinical audit but they are focused on measuring the effectiveness of clinical procedures. The measures of effectiveness are often focused only on clinical outcomes and the performance of staff but they can include a broader range of measures such as cost and staff time involved.

All the audit techniques start with a defined standard or norm of performance. These standards can be derived from research evidence or from expert opinion. Actual performance is then compared to this defined standard. Deficiencies are identified and action taken to remedy them. The effects of the action are then monitored to measure their effect. In many instances, clinical audit is now being used to develop protocols of performance to enable improvements to be sustained and for practice to be developed through inquiry.

As an approach, clinical audit can help to bring out into the open debates within a multi-disciplinary team about service priorities and the weight that should be attached to different variables. However, because they are targeted clearly at the overall improvement of patient care, they provide a structure for these debates which is practical rather than theoretical.

PUNS and STUNS

PUNS (Patient Unmet Needs) and STUNS (Staff Unmet Needs) is a critical incident analysis approach which my colleague Louise Buckle and I developed from some work originally carried out by Dr Richard Eve. PUNS and STUNS was developed for use in general practice but the approach would work in any setting.

The process works by asking staff in a meeting to give examples they have seen where a patient has had an unmet need as a result of the way the practice was organized or because of the knowledge of staff. The underlying causes are then discussed and actions are agreed to rectify them. For example, a practice receptionist attempted to put a call from a patient through to the practice nurse. The nurse did not answer the phone when she was dealing with a patient. The receptionist knows the nurse is in her room and is mystified why the phone just rings and rings. In this practice, for a variety of reasons no full practice meeting had been held for several months. The PUNS and STUNS process enabled the receptionist and nurse to sort out the problem. Neither was to blame. Both were trying to do the best for the patient they were dealing with at the time. The agreement that in future messages would be taken for the practice nurse so that she could return the calls at the end of her surgery was written down.

This recording on paper of the incident, the analysis and the actions resulting are an important part of the PUNS and STUNS process. It is a good way of validating the knowledge of staff and over a period of months it is possible to see the patterns that emerge from the PUNS and STUNS. This makes it possible to look at specific development programmes involving recurring problems.

Peer review

Peer review is a process where the practice of an individual or group of practitioners is reviewed by an individual or group who are from the same profession or background. It gives individual practitioners the opportunity to have their practice put under the microscope by someone who is expert in their field. The result can be a searching examination. Peer review is a way of validating practice and of ensuring that you are keeping up with professional standards.

In the context of a multi-disciplinary team this can be a strength and a weakness. Its advantage is that practitioners are often isolated from their professional colleagues when working within a multi-disciplinary setting. It can be refreshing and invigorating to explore your particular area of expertise with a colleague who shares your expertise and enthusiasm. The disadvantage is that it can reinforce the uni-disciplinary nature of most professional training and education. Being a professional in a genuinely multi-disciplinary team is different from being one in a uni-disciplinary team.

Shadowing

Shadowing is a technique which is particularly useful if you are trying to understand the role of a colleague and the constraints they are operating under. As such, it can be particularly useful for a multi-disciplinary team, especially in the early stages when individuals are still trying to understand the roles of their colleagues.

It consists of following someone (being their shadow) around for a day or a week and observing them at work. You will see the pressures they are under and have the opportunity to talk through why they handled issues in the way they did rather than any other way.

Shadowing makes it much easier to put yourself in the other person's shoes. You will come away with a much better insight into the practical pressures and dilemmas which colleagues are facing. It is time-consuming, but can give powerful insights.

360-degree feedback

This process, 360-degree feedback, takes the normal management appraisal process which we discussed in Chapter 5 and extends it to all staff involved with the person being appraised. The individual gets feedback not only from their boss but also from their peers in the team and others with whom they are in contact. If they are in a management position the staff who report to them also have the opportunity to give feedback. In short, the feedback comes from all directions: above, below and sideways.

Most people's initial response is to throw their hands up in horror at the thought of the people who are their peers or managed by them commenting on their performance. In fact, provided the process is well structured, the benefits of getting a rounded picture are considerable. The purpose of management is to manage people and who is better able to comment on your management style than the people receiving it?

Hearing the messages about your style from colleagues and particularly staff you manage can be odd at first, much like when you first hear your voice on a tape recorder. What the world thinks you sound like and what you think you sound like are two very different things.

For a multi-disciplinary team, 360-degree feedback can provide powerful insights into how effectively the team is operating as a whole. Have the professional boundaries been broken down? Are people clear about what they are supposed to be doing and what their role is? Do they feel part of a team? And so on.

Field-books

All of the techniques above rely on the collection of data to make them work. A field-book, sometimes called a logbook, is a notebook you use for all your notes of all your meetings, your action plans, ideas that suddenly come to you, neat one-liners that people have used. Instead of having all these notes on separate bits of paper that inevitably get lost or scrunched up, they are all in one place. I use wiro-bound A4 hardback notebooks which you can fold back on themselves. I know that whatever I want will be in there. If I jot down someone's phone number it goes in the book, I make Christmas present lists in my notebook. Everything goes in my notebook. I date most of the entries and when I have finished a notebook I put a sticky label on the front with the dates the notebook covers. This means I can then use my diary as an index. Earlier this week I was looking for my notes of a meeting with a colleague. I knew I saw Yvonne in October of last year, I checked my diary for the exact date and found the notes of the meeting in my field-book straight away.

For me my field-books give me the simplest data recording systems imaginable. I can jot everything down safe in the knowledge it won't get lost and I get interesting clashes which spark things off in my mind. I might be browsing through looking for the draft agenda of a meeting with a general practice and find a note I made of a meeting with a health authority from another part of the country which was pertinent to the agenda. Over a longer period of time the material in my fiel-books gives me a measure of my own development.

When I started writing this book I ploughed back through all eight years'-worth of my field-books and unearthed a lot of material which I have used. During that search I found a note of a meeting I attended in the autumn of 1990 when I was doing some research on health authorities after the purchaser-provider split. It was a project I was completely stuck with at the time. Written down were three questions suggested by a colleague which I remember at the time representing for me a major breakthrough. When I looked at them again they seemed obvious and I wondered why I was in such a mess with that project. And then I realized how much I had developed since then.

Making Your Choice

It is always worth seeking advice from your personnel and HR specialists. The following questions will help you to decide which method is likely to give the best results for you.

- Is the learning need personal to you or do other colleagues share it?
- How much time do you have?
- How much money is available?
- Do you need to learn a new skill or acquire new knowledge or do you want to think about and reflect on your work?
- What learning and training methods have you found particularly helpful in the past? What was it that made them so useful to you?

When making your choice, you need to bear in mind finding the right balance between deepening your knowledge about one particular area (becoming more expert) and setting that specific knowledge into a larger context (becoming more generalist). Being a reflective practitioner is not simply a question of acquiring more hard knowledge. To be a really effective manager, particularly of a multi-disciplinary team, you have to become wiser.

Conclusion

As a reflective practitioner you have to manage the links between the following:

- your work and your learning;
- you and your colleagues;
- theory and practice;
- your work and your life;
- your learning and your work;
- this job and the next one;
- the needs of your users and the needs of the taxpayers;
- your staff and your organization;
- your work and your family.

As a manager you have to ensure that this happens for you, for the individual members of your team and the team as a whole. It is a complex mix. People learn in a discontinuous, lumpy way. Periods of confusion and depression when old understandings no longer work can be suddenly lit up by a new insight. I once tried to work out what sort of picture would describe this process. I drew arrows and boxes then tried squiggles and circles. I struggled with it for days and in the end I gave up. A couple of days later while watching a film on television I realized it would be a picture that changed colour. So be gentle on yourself. There are dozens of other pressures in your life. When the learning is ready it will come, provided you keep chipping away at it. Organize your learning as you would any other part of your job and you and your team will get there.

Chapter 11

Multi-agency Working

Introduction

Multi-agency working is becoming increasingly important in health and social care. There is a greater understanding of the value of treating people close to or in their own homes and the interconnections between the services received by individual patients. An elderly confused person can be cared for in their own home with a combination of meals on wheels, domiciliary care and regular contacts with members of the primary health care team. This is both cheaper than placing the person in a nursing or residential home and helps to maintain a sense of independence and worth.

Multi-agency co-operation is the mainstay of many 'volume' care operations, but it is equally as important for the more bespoke care packages for people with complex conditions. A person who has, say, a learning disability may be under a consultant in a community unit, attending a sheltered work project run by a voluntary organization and being cared for day to day at home by his or her parents with the support of social services. Each agency provides a part of the package of care. It is the combination and integration of the elements that make the care package effective.

Many of the themes about communication, developing trust, integrating different perspectives of care run through multi-agency work, but there are some differences. This chapter discusses these differences and the issues that flow from them. It concludes by identifying the principles of successful multi-agency working.

Differences Between Agencies

The legal framework

There is a common-sense view of health and social care that it is all public money, we are all committed to providing high-quality services to patients and users and therefore everything should be shared. There is much in this. As far as users are concerned, they have paid their taxes and are rightly unimpressed by conflicts between agencies over roles and responsibilities. Moreover, they can be confused by the myriad of professionals arriving on their doorstep often in groups of three or four.

As taxpayers we are concerned that our money is being well spent. How that money can be spent is prescribed by the legal framework which defines the rights of public agencies to intervene in our lives. This legal framework has emerged piecemeal over the last 100 years as successive governments have initiated, strengthened and reversed policies on local government, the health service, pensions, housing, education and the rest of the welfare state. The result is a tangled web of law which empowers agencies to work in particular ways with particular groups and lays down how those agencies will account for their actions.

The outcome of this process is simply stated. Different agencies are accountable to different people for different things. These differences can work themselves out in apparently trivial disputes. The classic example is the endlessly debated question about bathing an elderly person at home: is it a social care bath or a health bath? But lying behind this apparently trivial issue is the fundamental question of the legal boundaries of the organizations concerned.

Cost shunting and incentives

Now add to the legal patchwork an era of scarce resources and the game can become redefining patients and users so that they fall into someone else's area of responsibility. Thus we get 'them' to pay for as much as possible so that we can spend more of 'our' budget on other badly needed services. This is known as cost shunting. The position has been further complicated by the application of incentives in the system. These have been designed to deliver particular policy outcomes, for example, to close long-stay mental institutions. But typically these incentives have been developed in isolation and without looking at the wider impact they will have on the total system of care. The result is an array of incentives which cut across each other reinforcing the different agendas that agencies are working to.

Trevor Hadley and Matt Muijjen in an article in the *Health Service Journal* in 1995 looked at the financial incentives operating at that time on health authorities, local authorities and GPs in the provision of community care for people with severe mental health problems. They summarized their argument in the table below. A plus sign indicates the incentives encouraging the stakeholder to increase use of this type of resource. A minus sign indicates the incentives are encouraging the stakeholder to reduce use of this type of resource.

	Health Authorities	Local Authorities	GPs
Long-stay beds	−	+	+
Acute hospital beds	+	−	−
Discharges	−	+	+
Admissions	−	+	+
Length of stay	+	+	+
CPNs	+	+	+
Social workers	+	−	+

This graphically demonstrates the way financial incentives for three key stakeholders are in conflict with each other. The result is the undermining of an integrated community care for seriously mentally ill people, the direct opposite of the stated policies of the three stakeholders and the Government. Hadley and Muijjen conclude that incentives should be developed which encourage co-operation and integration rather than fragmentation.

(Reproduced by kind permission of the
Editor of the *Health Service Journal*)

Culture

The legislative framework underpins some of the differences in culture which mark agencies working in health and social care. I worked in local government for a number of years before I moved to a job in the NHS. After about three months of trying to puzzle out this strange new beast I was working in I remember concluding that the NHS was just another large public bureaucracy. It took me about another six months to realize I was hopelessly wrong and that I had no idea how the NHS worked. It was probably another two years before I began to get a real sense of the NHS culture and how the system really worked.

These differences in culture are fundamental and colour all parts of the relationship between the NHS and local authorities. They stem from a number of reasons:

- the vastness of the NHS accountable to the Secretary of State in Parliament against the local ward accountability of local authorities;
- the entrenched power of the professions within the NHS;
- the authority of elected members to intervene at any level of local government activity.

The list goes on. The point is that people working in the NHS and local government are generally unaware of these differences. For example, staff in the NHS rarely understand the way all local government actions are examined through the lens of ward level politics. Likewise, local government staff rarely understand the power struggles between branches of medicine.

Confidentiality

For many professionals working in the NHS the issue of confidentiality arises when working with staff from other agencies. This is often used as an argument against joint notes on patients, even where such arrangements can facilitate improved communication across organizational boundaries. The general expectation is that information provided by a patient will remain confidential unless the patient gives their consent or disclosure can be justified in the wider public interest.

The wider public interest is usually taken to mean the interest of an individual, of groups of individuals or society as a whole and would, for example, encompass such matters as serious crime, child abuse or drug trafficking. Sometimes the pertinent information relates not to the specific user whose case is under review, for example, a child in a child protection conference, but another family member who may be the subject of the allegation of abuse.

Often the issue of confidentiality is actually an expression of a lack of trust in partners from other agencies to maintain the patient's confidentiality. The issue of confidentiality can be a useful litmus test, both of the state of knowledge that partners have about each other's responsibilities but also the general health of the collaboration.

Language

These differences in agenda and culture articulate themselves in different languages. In Chapter 7 I have already discussed the role of language in helping to define groups and therefore divide off people from the rest of the world. This process is repeated in multi-agency settings and is further complicated by the same words being used to mean different things.

Some years ago I was running a joint planning day for a city-wide Social Services Department and the NHS Trust which covered the northern half of the city. Social Services had just restructured themselves into a purchaser-provider system. The new structure had been explained to one of the Trust managers who attended the regular liaison meeting between the two NHS Trusts and Social Services. During the planning day he took the opportunity to explain the new social service structure to a Trust colleague. Watched by an Assistant Director from Social Services, who had also attended the liaison meeting, he drew an organization chart. 'This,' he said, pointing to the left-hand side of the diagram, 'is the commissioning team and on the right are the providers.' At which point the Assistant Director interrupted. 'No, no. It's the other way. The purchasers are on the right-hand side and the providers on the left.' 'But these are provider job titles,' said the Trust manager. 'No, they're not,' said the man from Social Services, 'they're purchasers.' It later transpired that the representative from the Trust that covered the southern half of the city had also left the liaison meeting with the organization chart the wrong way round. Same words, different meanings.

Tempo

Finally, agencies differ in the speed at which they operate. Local authorities are governed by the cycle of committee meetings at which all major decisions are taken. It usually takes six to eight weeks to complete the cycle. The NHS works at a much quicker tempo. Managers in the NHS have much more licence to take decisions and to implement new policies than their local government colleagues. It is a moot point which provides the best services and value for money for people. The real point is that these different metabolic rates can cause real frustration if they are not recognized and worked with.

The Practicalities of Multi-agency Working

In practical terms, there are two major differences between working in a multi-agency context and working in a single agency context. These are managing without authority, and time and logistics.

Managing without authority

At first sight different employing organizations should not make that much difference to the way teams of professionals work together. However, it means that decisions can only be reached and enforced through negotiation and influence. The sanctions or threat of sanctions which are normally available to managers managing their own staff are extremely limited in a multi-agency context. This places great emphasis on the skill of managers to be able to steer a path through the conflicting agendas, cultures and languages we have just discussed. Moreover, these managers need to be able to find ways of reconciling the differences and not allowing decision-making to fall to the satisficing level of 'anything we can all agree to' but to continue to be driven by the delivery of high quality responsive services. The agreements that are struck need to work for the individual partners and for the system as a whole.

Influencing styles

There are many different ways of trying to influence someone to follow your way of thinking. I set out below just five. You may find that you are particularly attracted to one above the others, but all of us use most of these styles at one time or another depending on the circumstances. The styles are:

- detailed evidence;
- action-oriented;
- people benefits;
- future-building;
- value-driven.

The detailed evidence approach is based on the provision of high quality empirical data in support of your argument. You need to convince your partner that your evidence is accurate and precise and that the conclusions you have drawn are accurate and logical. Your position will need to be thoroughly thought through and you should have all the details at your fingertips.

The action-oriented approach is based on decisive, quick actions which are to the point and will be productive. You will need to convince your partner that the actions you propose are credible and relevant to the issue at hand. The benefits will need to be tangible and concrete. You will need to demonstrate your experience and commitment to the plan of action.

The people benefits approach emphasizes the care that you take of the people involved in the situation. Your partner will need to feel that the action is helpful and harmonizing the efforts of those involved. The benefits will be personal. You will need to show your loyalty and commitment to support the individuals concerned.

The future-building approach is based on creating a vision of the future which is desirable and necessary and towards which your actions will move the situation. Your partner will need you to explore and question the present situation and the desired future state and for you to demonstrate your originality and creativity. The benefits of your proposal will be innovative and global. You will need to demonstrate your flexibility and ability to cope with the unexpected.

The value-driven approach is based on a set of fundamental values which your partner can affirm. Your partner will need to feel that the action you propose is ethical and in line with the values you are jointly espousing. The benefits will be equitable. You will need to show your commitment in action to the values that you are espousing.

Five different starting points and five different ways of seeking to influence someone to your way of thinking. Initially you may choose the style most likely to influence you. Perhaps you are more likely to be swayed by facts or the opportunity to get stuck into something. However, you are trying to influence your partner so choose the approach which is most likely to ring bells for them.

Partnership working between agencies is a two-way street and your partner may be trying to influence you round to their way of thinking. There always has to be a degree of give and take in any partnership arrangement. In working out these compromises you and your partner need to be aware what the deal-busters are for your respective organizations. That is those things which your organization must have or cannot possibly agree to.

Running through multi-agency work is a tension largely absent from single-agency work. This is the tension between autonomy of the multi-agency group to take decisions that will impact on all agencies within the system and accountability of the individual members back to their individual employing organizations. One of the commonest causes of failure within multi-agency teams is the reaching of decisions which the individual team members cannot deliver back in their own agency. As we have seen with the Hadley and Muijjen example, what seems highly plausible when viewed in a multi-agency context can sometimes look heavily one-sided when examined by individual agencies. It becomes easy at this point to denigrate the work of individuals who are perceived to have sold out the interests of our agency or profession. Getting two or more large public bureaucracies to run in step is no easy task.

The search for win-win solutions can be a taxing one and demands that managers understand their partners. As I have noted before, it is hard to work with strangers. Investing the time to get to know your partners and in particular to understand the constraints they are operating under will be repaid. As I have also argued before, the key to success is to meet people on their own ground and within their own mind-set. There are a number of ways this can be improved. For example, by doing the following:

- running joint training programmes;
- running joint induction programmes;
- setting up cross-agency mentoring and shadowing schemes.

Time and logistics

It is here that we meet the second practical issue in multi-agency working: that of time and logistics. The apparently simple task of getting everyone in the same room at the same time can absorb disproportionate amounts of administrative time. Once there, multi-agency work can often be undermined by the continual change of faces sitting around the table. Multi-agency teams have to go through the same forming, norming, storming and performing process as any internal team. Without a commitment to continuity, the team can constantly find itself back at square one. This can be a real practical difficulty. If an agency is short of staff as a result of workload pressures, staff vacancies or sickness, an 'external' meeting will often appear less important than providing the service. There is no doubt that an organization's ability to cope with the demands of multi-agency working fluctuates. Sometimes it is predictable, March is always bad, sometimes it is just events that overwhelm the best intentions.

Even with the same people in the room consistently, decisions often need to be referred back for validation and agreement from the home agency. This inevitably delays the decision-making process, particularly if agencies come back with comments or items they want clarification on. This can be particularly frustrating if it is not anticipated. The convoy can only go as fast as the slowest ship. A good rule of thumb to adopt is to estimate the time it would take the get the decision taken in one agency and then triple it. Multi-agency working always takes longer than people expect.

A NHS Trust and Social Services Department decided to jointly plan and deliver their community care training programme. To plan the programme, they invited 50 of the key local players with an interest in community care to a one-day conference at the start of the year. Each of the major agencies made a presentation on new initiatives they were planning for the year and the issues they would like the joint training programme to address. This enabled the conference to develop a picture of the world of community care and how it was likely to change in the coming year and the demands that would be made on staff. The second half of the day was spent identifying and agreeing the main topics the joint training programme should address. A small inter-agency steering group with representatives from each of the main sectors was formed and tasked with putting the detail onto the main topics and agreeing and organizing the delivery of the programme. The programme itself was so successful that the agencies agreed to repeat the process the following year.

There are ways of overcoming these problems. The case study illustrates one. Many agencies are now making increasing use of e-mail and other forms of electronic communication to progress multi-agency working.

Principles of Successful Multi-agency Working

It is possible to identify a number of features which characterize successful multi-agency partnerships.

- Reciprocity – reciprocity is the heart of all partnerships. There has to be something in it for all the partners or the partnership will fail. The benefits don't have to be symmetrical, although that helps.

- A convener – successful partnerships often have someone who plays the role of convener. This individual has respect across the agencies involved in the partnership and understands the issues as they affect the individual partners. They act almost as the physical embodiment of the partnership.
- The partnership works at all levels – the nuts and bolts of multi-agency agreements are often thrashed out by teams of middle managers. These agreements will come unstuck if they are not in tune with the thinking of senior management and cannot or will not be implemented by front-line staff. External agreements, particularly ones that we have not been a party to, often pose a direct threat to our sense of professional autonomy. The same managerial dilemmas about trading off involvement in the decision-making process against the time and cost it takes apply just as much in a multi-agency setting as they do in a multi-disciplinary setting.
- Successful multi-agency partnerships actively engage with the differences – just as multi-disciplinary teams bring together values and mind-sets which can be in conflict with each other, so do multi-agency teams. The solution is the same. Bring the differences out into the open and work with them honestly. Multi-agency and multi-disciplinary working are about managing the differences and getting the best from them.
- Working with structures – in the same way as the submerged world of values and mind-sets needs to be actively worked with, so does the surface world of structures and regulations. Multi-agency structures are often unwieldy and cumbersome. My own view is that, wherever possible, existing structures should be adapted rather than new ones constructed.
- Focus for progress – because of the difficulties in working in multi-agency contexts and reconciling contradictory incentives, cultures and agendas, there can be a tendency to float up into the balmy ether of warm words and mission statements which seem to say lot but do not actually add up to much. I have found that focusing in on specific projects and tasks helps to clarify the issues for agencies: is there anything in this for us at all? What are we prepared to put in order to receive the benefit? And so on.

Conclusion

As we have seen, multi-agency working replays many of the themes that we have looked at in managing multi-disciplinary teams. Many of the techniques and frameworks we considered when developing multi-disciplinary teams will work on the multi-agency stage. Breaking down the Berlin Wall that has developed between agencies working in health and social care is a major task for managers at all levels in all organizations. As a recent Government Green Paper put it 'connected problems need joined up solutions'.

Chapter 12

Afterword

On a number of occasions I have talked about the importance of having a development plan for your team. Such a plan acts as the single reference point which you can use to pull together your ideas about how you want your team to develop. I think that ideally this plan should not be longer than one side of an A4 sheet. To help you get started I set out below a series of questions which touch on the areas covered in this book. They will help you sort out what it is you want to do and what your priorities are. The techniques and frameworks set out in this book will help you put flesh on the bones.

- What are your goals for your multi-disciplinary team?
- What sort of culture do you want to develop within your team?
- What sort of culture do you want your team to perform?
- How will you motivate each of the members of your team and the team as a whole? What turns them on?
- How are you going to get the right mix of skills and experience in your team?
- How can you improve communication within the team, between the team and the rest of the organization, between the team and patients?
- What are your key five key messages?
- How are you going to develop the individuals within the team?
- How are you going to develop the team as a whole?
- How are you going to foster learning within the team?
- How are you going to develop yourself?
- If there was only one thing you could fix, what would it be?

Improving multi-disciplinary working to improve health care is one of the great challenges of the twenty-first century. I hope that you have found this book interesting and helpful. No short introduction like this can cover the full range of circumstances under which multi-disciplinary working in the NHS operates. I hope that I have at least given you some clues about how to start. If you have any comments on the book or the issues that it raises I would be delighted to hear from you. You can write to me at:

PRG Consultancy
1 Osborne Road
Southville
Bristol BS3 1PR

or e-mail me at paul@prgconsultancy.co.uk

References

Bridge Childcare Consultancy Service (1995) 'Paul, Death Through Neglect', Camden and Islington Area Child Protection Committee, London

Carers' National Association (1998) 'Ignored and Invisible?, Carers' Experience of the NHS', Carers' National Association, London

Downing, SJ (1997) Learning the plot: emotional momentum in search of dramatic logic, *Management Learning*, **28**, 1, pp 27–44

Hadley, T and Muijjen, M (1995) The incentivies war, *Health Service Journal*, 9 March

Henwood, M (1998) *Ignored and Invisible? Carers' Experience of the NHS*, Carers' National Association, London

Lippett, R (1983) Future before you plan, in R Ritvo and A Sargent (eds) *NTL Managers Handbook*, NTL Institute, Arlington, VA

McCann, JE and Gray, B (1986) Power and collaboration in human service domains, *International Journal of Sociology and Social Policy*, **6**, pp 58–67

McGregor, D (1960) *The Human Side of Enterprise*, McGraw-Hill, New York

Petrioni (1994) Interprofessional teamwork, in Leathard A, *Going Inter-professional*, Routledge, London

Lickert, R (1969) *The Human Organization*, McGraw-Hill, New York

Rhodes, J (1988) *The Colours of Your Mind*, HarperCollins, London

Schein, EH (1988) *Organizational Psychology*, Prentice Hall, London

Tuckman, B (1965) Development sequences in small groups, *Psychological Bulletin*, **63**, pp 384–99

Upton, T and Brooks, B (1995) *Managing Change in the NHS*, Kogan Page, London

West, M and Slater J (1996) *Teamworking in Primary Health Care*, Health Education Authority, London

Zaleznik, A (1977) Managers and leaders: are they different?, *Harvard Business Review*, May/June, pp 67–78

Zeiss, RA (1997) Interdisciplinary treatment and training issues in the acute inpatient psychiatry unit, *Journal of Interprofessional Care*, **11**, 3

Further Reading

Belbin, MR (1994) *Management Teams: Why They Succeed or Fail*, Butterworth-Heinemann, Oxford

Fisher, R and Ury, W (1991) *Getting to Yes*, Century, London

Furnham, A (1997) *The Pyschology of Behaviour at Work*, Psychology Press, Hove

Jones, MO (1996) *Studying Organizational Symbolism*, Sage, London

Kennedy, C (1991) *Guide to the Management Gurus*, Century, London

Morgan, G (1986) *Images of Organization*, Sage, London

Paton, R, Clark, G, Jones, G, Lewis, J and Quintas, P (eds) (1996) *The New Management Reader*, Routledge, London

Pedler, M, Burgoyne, J and Boydell, T (1991) *The Learning Company*, McGraw-Hill, Maidenhead

Sources of Help

The Centre for the Advancement of Inter-Professional Education (CAIPE) produce the *Journal of Interprofessional Care* which is a very valuable quarterly journal. For more details on membership and subscriptions call CAIPE on 0171 278 1083. There is also a linked web site at http://www.city.ac.uk/barts/jipc.htm

Jerry Rhodes' book can be ordered direct on Thunks@dial.pipex.com or 01453 521 585.

Index

Page references in italics indicate figures or tables